THE
GROWTH

OF AN EXPANDING MISSION

A STUDY OF **ACTS** 10:1 – 18:18

BIBLE STUDY GUIDE

From the Bible-teaching ministry of

Charles R. Swindoll

INSIGHT FOR LIVING

Charles R. Swindoll is a graduate of Dallas Theological Seminary and has served as senior pastor of the First Evangelical Free Church of Fullerton, California, since 1971. Chuck's radio program, "Insight for Living," began in 1979. In addition to his church and radio ministries, Chuck enjoys writing. He has authored numerous books and booklets on a variety of subjects.

Based on the outlines and transcripts of Chuck's sermons, the study guide text is co-authored by Bryce Klabunde, a graduate of Biola University and Dallas Theological Seminary. He also wrote the Living Insights sections.

Editor in Chief:
Cynthia Swindoll

Coauthor of Text:
Bryce Klabunde

Assistant Editor:
Wendy Peterson

Copy Editors:
Deborah Gibbs
Glenda Schlahta

Designer:
Gary Lett

Publishing System Specialist:
Bob Haskins

Director, Communications Division:
Deedee Snyder

Project Manager:
Alene Cooper

Project Supervisor:
Susan Nelson

Project Assistants:
Ellen Galey
Cheryl Gilmore

Print Production Manager:
John Norton

Printer:
Sinclair Printing Company

Unless otherwise identified, all Scripture references are from the New American Standard Bible, © The Lockman Foundation 1960, 1962, 1963, 1968, 1971, 1972, 1973, 1975, 1977. Used by permission. Scripture taken from the Holy Bible, New International Version, © 1973, 1978, 1984 International Bible Society, used by permission of Zondervan Bible Publishers. The other translation cited is The Living Bible [LB].

An effort has been made to locate sources and obtain permission where necessary for the quotations used in this book. In the event of any unintentional omission, a modification will gladly be incorporated in future printings.

ISBN 0-8499-8436-X
Printed in the United States of America.

COVER DESIGN: Jerry Ford
COVER PHOTOGRAPH: SuperStock, Inc.
TEXT ILLUSTRATION (chapter 1): Gary Lett

CONTENTS

INTRODUCTION

The rapid-fire story of Acts has been compared to a spreading flame. From an obscure, frightened group of Jews in a room at Jerusalem, a worldwide mission was launched that has never stopped. What started ever so small now reaches into Europe and, ultimately, far beyond the ancient boundaries of the Roman Empire. In that sense, Acts remains an unfinished account of spiritual growth and numerical expansion. The flame has, indeed, continued to spread.

This second volume of our study in Acts begins where the previous volume ended. Saul of Tarsus, now converted to Christ, emerges as the central figure of significance. He even overshadows the once-prominent Peter as he is sent on his first missionary journey with Barnabas . . . then, later, on his second journey with Silas. What a work God is doing! In the harshest of times and with the most primitive of tools and methods of travel, the mission expands. And in every place Paul travels, God's Word is proclaimed, resulting in the founding of churches and the writing of letters—many of which have become a part of the New Testament Scriptures.

It is our prayer that the Lord will use these studies to broaden your perspective and deepen your faith. God is still on the move. His sovereign plan continues to unfold, which includes this very day in which we live. And never forget . . . it includes *you*.

Chuck Swindoll .

PUTTING TRUTH INTO ACTION

Knowledge apart from application falls short of God's desire for His children. He wants us to apply what we learn so that we will change and grow. This study guide was prepared with these goals in mind. As you go through the following pages, we hope your desire to discover biblical truth will grow as your understanding of God's Word increases, and that you will be encouraged to apply what you've learned.

To assist you in your study, we've included a section called ⦿ **Living Insights** at the end of each lesson. These exercises will challenge you to study further and to think of specific ways to put your discoveries into action.

There are many ways to use this guide—in personal devotions, group studies, discussions with friends and family, and Sunday school classes. And, of course, it's an ideal study aid when you're listening to its corresponding "Insight for Living" radio series.

To benefit most from this study guide, we would encourage you to consider it a spiritual journal. That's why we've included space in the **Living Insights** for recording your thoughts and discoveries. We hope you'll return to those sections often for review and encouragement as you continue to grow in your walk with Christ.

Bryce Klabunde

Bryce Klabunde
Coauthor of Text
Author of Living Insights

THE

GROWTH

OF AN EXPANDING MISSION

A STUDY OF **ACTS** 10:1 – 18:18

ACTS: THE SPREADING FLAME

Writer: Dr. Luke
Theme: The growth of the early church
Key Verse: Acts 1:8
Major People: Peter and Paul
Central Locations: Jerusalem and Antioch
Prediction Fulfilled: "I will build my church. . . ." (Matt. 16:18)

A Book of Origins:
- Coming of the Holy Spirit
- Beginning of the church and the gifts of the Spirit
- Apostolic authority
- Outbreak of persecution/martyrdom
- World missions
- Grace instead of Law

	The Church Established at Jerusalem*	The Church Scattered to Judea and Samaria*	The Church Extended to "Remotest Part"*
	The church is . . .	The gospel is . . .	The witness is . . .
	. . . born	. . . spreading	. . . extended
	. . . tested	. . . multiplying	. . . received and rejected
	. . . purified	. . . changing lives	. . . unifying Jews and Gentiles
	. . . strengthened	. . . breaking traditions	
	A.D. 30		A.D. 60
Chapter Numbers	1 7	8 12	13 28
Leaders	The Apostle Peter		The Apostle Paul
Emphasis	Mainly Jews	Mixing Jews and Gentiles	Mainly Gentiles
Time	2 years	13 years	15 years
Scope	City Evangelism	Home Missions	Foreign Missions

*Main headings adapted from Irving L. Jensen, *Acts: An Independent Study* (Chicago, Ill.: Moody Press, 1968), p. 52.

Chapter 1

FACING THE PRIDE-PREJUDICE SINDROME

Acts 10:1–23a

In the spring of 1992, violence inflamed the city of Los Angeles. When the smoke finally cleared, an estimated 5,200 buildings were destroyed or damaged, and losses ranged close to $1 billion. A staggering number of people were arrested—almost 17,000. The number of injured soared to 2,383, and the death bell tolled a tragic 54 times.[1]

What could have fueled such a destructive rampage?

In speculating about the many possible causes for the riots, we can sift through the city's rubble and uncover a major flash point—prejudice. Differences in color and culture had ignited misunderstanding, which had sparked antagonism, which had inflamed hatred, then anger, then revenge. The result was thirty-six hours of havoc and bloodshed.

We shake our heads at such horrible violence, but admit it or not, we all have that same volatile prejudice smoldering within us. According to *Webster's*, prejudice is simply a "preconceived judgment."[2] Do you see in yourself a tendency to prejudge others?

Take a moment for a quick personal prejudice test. What images come to mind when you think of blacks or whites or Hispanics or Asians? How about those who are poor? Or those who are wealthy? Do you categorize people by the length of their hair or the cosmetics they wear or don't wear? Politically, what about liberals? Conservatives? How do you feel about people who have failed? Who are

1. Eloise Salholz, with Lynda Wright and Rebecca Crandall, "A New Challenge for Ueberroth," *Newsweek*, May 18, 1992, p. 45.

2. *Webster's Ninth New Collegiate Dictionary*, see "prejudice."

1

divorced? Who've been in psychiatric hospitals?

What about religious prejudices? How do you view those who attend a different church? Who worship differently than you do? Or who have a different list of do's and don'ts?

It's painful to face our own prejudices. And like being trapped in a smoke-filled building, it's hard to see through the negative preconceptions we've had all our lives. We're not alone, however, for the apostle Peter was trapped by prejudice too. Let's watch how God rescues him as we begin this second volume of our study of the book of Acts.

A Brief Orientation

In Acts 1–7, the church was born and established in Jerusalem. Opposition to the gospel soon arose, however—Stephen was stoned, and in chapters 8–9, a wave of persecution scattered the believers into Judea and Samaria. As they went, they preached the gospel to the Samaritan Jews, and the church grew even more.

Our study begins during this period of scattering, about A.D. 40, less than a decade after Christ's crucifixion and the coming of the Holy Spirit.[3] Peter, at this time, resided in Joppa at the house of Simon the tanner.

Joppa was a seaside town, located about thirty miles south of Caesarea, where a certain Gentile named Cornelius lived. More than just miles separated Cornelius and Peter, however. As a Jew, Peter was taught throughout his life to despise people like Cornelius. Alfred Edersheim describes the extent of the inbred prejudice that Jews held against Gentiles.

> Every Gentile child, so soon as born, was to be re-
> garded as unclean. . . . The Mishnah goes so far as
> to forbid aid to a [Gentile] mother in the hour of
> her need, or nourishment to her babe, in order not
> to bring up a child for idolatry! . . .
>   . . . It was not safe to leave cattle in their
> charge, to allow their women to nurse infants, or
> their physicians to attend the sick, nor to walk in
> their company. . . . They and theirs were defiled;
> their houses unclean, as containing idols or things

---

3. See H. Wayne House, *Chronological and Background Charts of the New Testament* (Grand Rapids, Mich.: Zondervan Publishing House, Academie Books, 1981), p. 129.

dedicated to them; their feasts, their joyous occa-
sions, their very contact, was polluted by idolatry;
and there was no security, if a heathen were left
alone in a room, that he might not . . . defile the
wine or meat on the table, or the oil and wheat in
the store. . . . Milk drawn by a heathen, if a Jew
had not been present to watch it, bread and oil
prepared by them, were unlawful. Their wine was
wholly interdicted—the mere touch of a heathen
polluted a whole cask; nay, even to put one's nose
to heathen wine was strictly prohibited![4]

Because of his Jewish background, Peter probably had these
prejudicial sentiments lingering like a foul odor in his mind. Only
a fresh breath of God's grace could clear the air and open wide the
church's door to a world of Gentiles waiting to follow Christ. That
refreshing breeze came unexpectedly, when God brought Cornelius
and Peter face to face in a supernatural way.

A Divine Intervention

Cornelius was the first to experience the divine nudge that
brought the two men together. Luke introduces him in Acts 10:1–2.

A Gentile Named Cornelius

Now there was a certain man at Caesarea named
Cornelius, a centurion of what was called the Italian
cohort, a devout man, and one who feared God with
all his household, and gave many alms to the Jewish
people, and prayed to God continually.

As a centurion, Cornelius commanded one hundred soldiers
who were part of a Roman cohort or a battalion. Bearing his many
battle scars like medals, this tough military officer also wore the
honorable badge of a God-fearing man. Most Romans were poly-
theistic—worshiping many gods. But Cornelius chose to serve the
one God of the Jews, not only in word but in deed as well. He was
not a Christian at this time, but he was a seeker, sincerely desiring
to follow God. And God honored his devotion, enlisting him as

---

4. Alfred Edersheim, *The Life and Times of Jesus the Messiah* (1971; reprint, Grand Rapids,
Mich.: William B. Eerdmans Publishing Co., 1980), pp. 90–92.

the first in "the vanguard of the great army of Gentiles that soon entered the church."[5]

> About the ninth hour of the day he clearly saw in a vision an angel of God who had just come in to him, and said to him, "Cornelius!" And fixing his gaze upon him and being much alarmed, he said, "What is it, Lord?" And he said to him, "Your prayers and alms have ascended as a memorial before God. And now dispatch some men to Joppa, and send for a man named Simon, who is also called Peter; he is staying with a certain tanner named Simon, whose house is by the sea." (vv. 3–6)

A well-trained soldier, Cornelius didn't ask why; he just immediately obeyed the Lord's orders and sent some men to Joppa to bring Peter back (vv. 7–8).

Peter, however, knew nothing of Cornelius' vision or the men coming to find him . . . until God gave him a vision of his own.

A Jew Named Peter

While Cornelius' men journeyed to Joppa, the Lord had time to speak to Peter. Around noon the next day, the Apostle went up to the housetop to pray.

> And he became hungry, and was desiring to eat; but while they were making preparations, he fell into a trance; and he beheld the sky opened up, and a certain object like a great sheet coming down, lowered by four corners to the ground, and there were in it all kinds of four-footed animals and crawling creatures of the earth and birds of the air. And a voice came to him, "Arise, Peter, kill and eat!" (vv. 10–13)

Poor Peter was famished, and here the Lord gave him a vision of food! God was using his hunger and an eyeful of victuals to teach Peter a life-changing lesson.

Now, Jews were proud of how they kept God's Old Testament dietary laws, which forbade them to eat foods deemed "unclean."

---

5. R. C. H. Lenski, *The Interpretation of the Acts of the Apostles* (Columbus, Ohio: Wartburg Press, 1944), p. 393.

So as Peter looked over this spread of clean and unclean animals and heard God say, "Kill and eat," he cringed. "By no means, Lord," he exclaimed, "for I have never eaten anything unholy and unclean" (v. 14).

Unlike Cornelius, who obeyed right away, Peter blurted out an objection, which actually amounted to a contradiction in terms. "By no means, Lord," Peter said. But if Christ was truly his Lord, Peter would never have said no to Him. Peter's pride was submarining his devotion to the Master.

So the voice spoke back: "What God has cleansed, no longer consider unholy" (v. 15b).

God's grace had flung open the tightly closed doors of legalism: Christ's atonement had cleansed the unholy so that all people could be accepted by Him. But would proud Peter understand the true meaning of the vision?

According to verse 16, the Lord had to show Peter the vision three times, and still "Peter was greatly perplexed in mind as to what the vision which he had seen might be" (v. 17a). How many times must God expose our prejudices before we learn that all people are equal before Him?

Alexander Whyte echoes God's strong indictment.

> All mankind, indeed, except Peter and a few of his friends, were bound up together in one abominable bundle. And Peter was standing above them, scouting at and spitting on them all. All so like ourselves. For, how we also bundle up whole nations of men and throw them into that same unclean sheet. Whole churches that we know nothing about but their bad names that we have given them, are in our sheet of excommunication also. All the other denominations of Christians in our land are common and unclean to us. Every party outside of our own party in the political state also. . . . They are four-footed beasts and creeping things. Indeed, there are very few men alive, and especially those who live near us, who are not sometimes in the sheet of our scorn.[6]

6. Alexander Whyte, *Bible Characters from the New Testament*, (New Canaan, Conn.: Keats Publishing, 1982), vol. 2, p. 36.

Who is in the "sheet of our scorn"? Someone of a different color or culture? Someone with a past or lifestyle foreign to ours? God accepts them through Christ. When will we accept them also?

A Gentile-Jew Encounter

God's message stings, doesn't it? Our prejudices are ugly, and how we hate for God to throw light on them. But for us to change, He must expose and even force them out into the open. God provided such an opportunity for Peter when three men came knocking at the gate.

> The men who had been sent by Cornelius, having asked directions for Simon's house, appeared at the gate; and calling out, they were asking whether Simon, who was also called Peter, was staying there. And while Peter was reflecting on the vision, the Spirit said to him, "Behold, three men are looking for you. But arise, go downstairs, and accompany them without misgivings; for I have sent them Myself." (vv. 17b–20)

"Why would I have misgivings?" Peter must have thought to himself. "Unless . . . unless these men are unclean Gentiles!" Now the vision began to make sense for Peter. But would he accept these Gentiles as the Lord had wanted him to accept the unclean animals in the sheet?

> Peter went down to the men and said, "Behold, I am the one you are looking for; what is the reason for which you have come?" And they said, "Cornelius, a centurion, a righteous and God-fearing man well spoken of by the entire nation of the Jews, was divinely directed by a holy angel to send for you to come to his house and hear a message from you." And so he invited them in and gave them lodging. (vv. 21–23a)

Peter, a Jew, gave lodging to Gentiles. In so doing, he passed the test.

A Practical Reaction

In the next lesson, we'll follow Peter to Cornelius' house. But for now, let's reflect on three principles that God has taught us in this passage so far.

First, *the root of prejudice is pride.* Pride sticks out its chest and struts around with a heart that shouts, "My way is the only way!" But this attitude grows the rancid fruit of prejudice. And when we ridicule others for their different ways, frankly, our sin turns God's stomach.

Second, *the resistance in prejudice is brought on by tradition, not Scripture.* Our parents, our peers, our culture are often the mentors of our prejudices. Peter had been weaned on hatred for Gentiles. In our own families, we must uproot the traditions that lead us to prejudge others because of our differences.

Third, *facing the wrong of prejudice is painful.* As the pages of the calendar flip by and the years pass, prejudices become more and more embedded in our lives. And just as it's painful to dig out a thorn that has set itself deeply under our skin, so it is equally difficult to remove prejudice. But if by the power of the Holy Spirit Peter could wrest it out of his life, then by that same power so can we.

 Living Insights

Alexander Whyte prescribes a healing but painful procedure to treat the disease of prejudice in our hearts.

> If you would take a four-cornered napkin . . . and write the names of the nations, and the churches, and the denominations, and the congregations, and the ministers, and the public men, and the private citizens, and the neighbours, and the fellow-worshippers,—all the people you dislike, and despise, and do not, and cannot, and will not, love. Heap all their names into your unclean napkin, and then look up and say, "Not so, Lord. I neither can speak well, nor think well, nor hope well, of these people. I cannot do it, and I will not try." If you acted out and spake out all the evil things that are in your heart in some such way as that, you would thus get such a sight of yourselves that you would never forget it.[7]

7. Whyte, *Bible Characters from the New Testament,* p. 37.

Imagine the following square as your four-cornered napkin, the sheet that God has lowered before you. As Whyte suggested, write down a list of your "unclean" people.

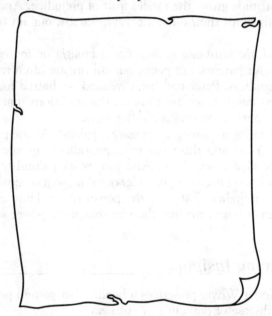

Now, as Whyte prescribed, voice the words that have been in your heart for so long. Listen to them spoken from your own lips: "Not so, Lord. I neither can speak well, nor think well, nor hope well, of these people. I cannot do it, and I will not try."

Does your prejudice look ugly before you? Can you not accept as brothers and sisters those for whom Christ has died? Pray that God will wipe clean your sheet of scorn, erasing the names one by one. Then you'll be able to proclaim Whyte's final words:

> "Of a truth I perceive that God is no respecter of persons. But in every nation, and church, and denomination, and party of men, and among those I used to think of as four-footed beasts of the earth, and wild beasts, and creeping things, God has them that fear Him, and that work righteousness, and that are accepted of Him."[8]

8. Whyte, *Bible Characters from the New Testament*, p. 37.

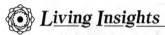

Prejudices are like cockroaches. Once we think they're gone, they creep back unnoticed, infesting the dark corners of our lives. It takes consistent maintenance to completely eliminate them.

As in changing any bad habit, we must first be aware of our prejudiced thoughts and words. In the previous Living Insight, we began to recognize them, but we must routinely catch our prejudices in action. Consider the following Prejudice Extermination Plan:

- This week, try to catch yourself every time you prejudge someone because of their differences. Simply being aware of your prejudices will help eradicate many of them.

- Next, associate negative images with prejudiced thoughts. When you hear a racial joke, imagine the hurt such ridicule would cause someone of that color or culture. Imagine your own feelings if you were the brunt of the joke.

- Then replace your prejudiced thoughts with positive thoughts. Find good in those at whom you once scoffed. Try foods from different cultures; listen to their music; read some of their books. Get to know your neighbors who seem so different than you, and remind yourself of God's gracious acceptance of them in Christ.

- Above all, pray for those on your sheet of scorn; seek with them God's forgiveness and salvation. Maybe the Lord will even give you a love for those you hate. Then you'll know that your prejudices are gone for good.

Chapter 2

GOD IS NOT PARTIAL

Acts 10:23b–48

Is God biased?

As a Jew, Peter might have thought so. After all, the priests who served Him were Jews, the prophets who proclaimed Him were Jews, and the scholars who described Him were Jews. They were God's "chosen people"—the guardians of His temple and His Law, the recipients of His covenants. Obviously, Israel was God's favorite. A superior nation . . . right?

God did have His heart set on the Jews—but not because they were greater or more righteous or more deserving than other nations. He chose them simply to demonstrate His grace and love for the entire world. In fact, an unbiased, impartial acceptance of all people had been His plan all along.

A Principle to Remember: Impartiality

James vividly illustrated God's impartiality by setting it against the dark backdrop of human favoritism.

> If a man comes into your assembly with a gold ring and dressed in fine clothes, and there also comes in a poor man in dirty clothes, and you pay special attention to the one who is wearing the fine clothes, and say, "You sit here in a good place," and you say to the poor man, "You stand over there, or sit down by my footstool," have you not made distinctions among yourselves, and become judges with evil motives? (James 2:2–4)

God hates this kind of partiality! It rankles Him when we prejudge people on the basis of appearances (see 1 Sam. 16:7). In fact, God told James to write that

> if you show partiality, you are committing sin and are convicted by the law as transgressors. (James 2:9)

The apostle Paul also showed God's stand against prejudice when he declared:

There is neither Jew nor Greek, there is neither slave nor free man, there is neither male nor female; for you are all one in Christ Jesus. (Gal. 3:28)

Through their words, James and Paul teach us the facts of impartiality. But it is through Peter's life, as we shall see next, that we'll learn how to live it.

A Case in Point: The Gentiles

Peter, as you'll recall from our previous lesson, had just met Cornelius' Gentile messengers at his own front door. Would he follow Jewish tradition and have nothing to do with these "unclean" people? Or would he heed the lesson God taught him through the vision?

Lesson learned, he invites them in . . .

Peter's Hospitality

Breaking age-old traditions of prejudice, Peter not only welcomes the visitors but also gives them lodging for the night (Acts 10:23a). Then, the following day, he does the unthinkable.

> He arose and went away with them, and some of the brethren from Joppa accompanied him. (v. 23b)

This is possibly the first time Peter has journeyed with Gentiles. As he walks the thirty miles from Joppa to Caesarea, what goes through his mind? "These Gentiles are human after all," he thinks, peering at them from the corner of his eye. "They're not so different. What have I been afraid of all these years?"

Peter's Humility

Sailing in the breeze of grace, Peter

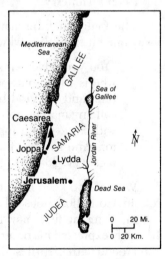

Peter's Ministry[1]

1. *Life Application® Bible*, New International Version (copublishers; Wheaton, Ill.: Tyndale House Publishers, 1991 and Grand Rapids, Mich.: Zondervan Publishing House, 1991), p. 1969. Maps © 1986, 1988 by Tyndale House Publishers, Inc. All rights reserved. Used by permission.

begins to delight in God's new heading for his life. His changing attitude especially shows itself when he arrives at Cornelius' house.

> When it came about that Peter entered, Cornelius met him, and fell at his feet and worshiped him. But Peter raised him up, saying, "Stand up; I too am just a man." (vv. 25–26)

Peter could have reveled in the centurion's adoration. After all, he is the chief apostle and a Jew; Gentile Cornelius is fortunate just to have him in his house. But by saying, "I too am just a man," Peter models humility—an essential quality in the family of Christ.

A church filled with humble Christians has an atmosphere of equality. One person is not more or less important than the next. It's like the children's clubhouse that had these words scribbled on its wall:

> Nobody act big.
> Nobody act small.
> Everybody act medium.[2]

Everybody act equal—a fitting rule for any church.

Peter's Honesty

The Galilean fisherman also models honesty in not backing away one bit from the awkwardness of the Gentile-Jew interaction.

> "You yourselves know how unlawful it is for a man who is a Jew to associate with a foreigner or to visit him; and yet God has shown me that I should not call any man unholy or unclean. That is why I came without even raising any objection when I was sent for. And so I ask for what reason you have sent for me." (vv. 28–29)

We need to keep in mind how uncomfortable Peter must have felt in Cornelius' house. Like an aquarium fish thrown into the ocean, Peter at first may have feared the freedom of grace. He honestly expressed his natural hesitation, quoting his old rule: Don't run around with Gentiles. But then, remembering that strange sheet and all the animals, he relayed Christ's principle of love: We should call no one unclean.

2. Eleanor L. Doan, comp., *The Speaker's Sourcebook* (Grand Rapids, Mich.: Zondervan Publishing House, 1960), p. 17.

Cornelius' Response

Cornelius, in explaining why he has sent for Peter, describes his own vision from the Lord (vv. 30–33a). Then, with an expectant pause, he concludes his story,

> "Now then, we are all here present before God to hear all that you have been commanded by the Lord." (v. 33b)

With that, all eyes focus on Peter.

A Message of Grace: Peace through Jesus

Gathering his thoughts, Peter crystallizes God's salvation plan for his receptive audience.

God and the Nations

His first point summarizes the shiny new truth the Lord has been teaching him about grace and divine impartiality.

> "I most certainly understand now that God is not one to show partiality, but in every nation the man who fears Him and does what is right, is welcome to Him. The word which He sent to the sons of Israel, preaching peace through Jesus Christ (He is Lord of all)." (vv. 34b–36)

Christ's spiritual peace is for everyone—"He is Lord of *all*," not just the Jews. Jesus has broken down the barriers and torn down the fences, and now He sends an invitation to all people to join His family (see also Rom. 3:28–30; Eph. 2:11–22).

God and Christ

After handing Jesus' invitation to this roomful of Gentiles, Peter then explains its contents: the gospel message.

> "You yourselves know the thing which took place throughout all Judea, starting from Galilee, after the baptism which John proclaimed. You know of Jesus of Nazareth, how God anointed Him with the Holy Spirit and with power, and how He went about doing good, and healing all who were oppressed by the devil; for God was with Him. And we are witnesses of all the things He did both in the land of the Jews

and in Jerusalem. And they also put Him to death by hanging Him on a cross. God raised Him up on the third day, and granted that He should become visible, not to all the people, but to witnesses who were chosen beforehand by God, that is, to us, who ate and drank with Him after He arose from the dead. And He ordered us to preach to the people, and solemnly to testify that this is the One who has been appointed by God as Judge of the living and the dead. Of Him all the prophets bear witness that through His name *everyone who believes in Him receives forgiveness of sins.*" (Acts 10:37–43, emphasis added)

Peter's words bathe Cornelius and his household in God's luxuriant grace. Jesus has poured out forgiveness, not just on a select few, but on anyone who believes—irrespective of culture, race, or station in life.

God and Salvation

Even as the Apostle speaks, his words wash over the spirits of the needy people, invigorating them with new life.

While Peter was still speaking these words, the Holy Spirit fell upon all those who were listening to the message. And all the circumcised believers who had come with Peter were amazed, because the gift of the Holy Spirit had been poured out upon the Gentiles also. For they were hearing them speaking with tongues and exalting God. Then Peter answered, "Surely no one can refuse the water for these to be baptized who have received the Holy Spirit just as we did, can he?" And he ordered them to be baptized in the name of Jesus Christ. Then they asked him to stay on for a few days. (vv. 44–48)

Just as the Holy Spirit had come upon Christ's followers at Pentecost, so He indwells these spiritually newborn Gentiles, and they immediately start speaking in tongues.[3] In this way, at this

---

3. In this situation, this miracle was an irrefutable sign to the Jews that God had accepted the Gentiles into the church. Today we should not suppose that the evidence for every conversion experience will be speaking in tongues, for even in the book of Acts, this event was unique.

unique historical juncture, God proves that His grace extends to everyone. All are welcome in Christ.

An Application for Today

Like Peter, we have our own boxes of prejudice made strong with religious regulations, cultural biases, and legalistic traditions. They are so sturdy, in fact, that it's difficult for us to break out of them or for anyone else to break in.

The story of Cornelius and Peter, however, teaches us a hopeful truth: there is *no one* the grace of God cannot liberate. Let God's grace free you from your prejudices today. Let it open up doors and windows in your life as it did in Peter's, so that the gospel message can pour out to a spiritually thirsty world.

 Living Insights

With the three-times-repeated vision and the events that followed, the Lord shook the foundation of Peter's judgmental attitude. Peter could have resisted God's hand, saying:

> "Gentiles will never change," or

> "Let me discuss this with the other apostles, and we'll get back to You," or

> "How about another sign, Lord?"

But instead, he said,

> "God has shown me that I should not call any man unholy or unclean," (v. 28b) and

> "I most certainly understand now that God is not one to show partiality." (v. 34b)

He opened his heart to the Lord and followed Him obediently.

What if the Lord pulled you away from your prejudices—would you be as teachable as Peter? In the following situations, honestly evaluate your willingness to accept others with Christ's love.

- A tattooed motorcycle gang member roars into the church parking lot one Sunday. The Lord tells you to welcome him into the service.

15

Resistance				Openness
1	2	3	4	5

- Some coworkers invite you to lunch at a bar. The Lord prompts you to go with them.

Resistance				Openness
1	2	3	4	5

- Your neighbors, who smoke heavily, need a place to live for a few days while workers repair their house. The Lord nudges you to invite them to stay with you.

Resistance				Openness
1	2	3	4	5

- The family who moves in next door has a teenage son with spiked hair, an earring, and army boots. The Lord encourages you to offer him rides to your church youth group.

Resistance				Openness
1	2	3	4	5

You can probably continue a list of situations drawn from your own life, where you've faced Cornelius-type people. Did God whisper in your ear that you should help them, but you reared back and resisted? If that happens in the future, remember one word . . . grace.

◉ Living Insights

Grace is memorably defined with an acrostic:

> God's
> Riches
> At
> Christ's
> Expense[4]

This definition pictures God with His pockets bulging, flinging handfuls of spiritual riches drawn on Christ's account to anyone who will receive them.

---

4. Ray Stedman, *Acts 1–12: Birth of the Body* (Santa Ana, Calif.: Vision House Publishers, 1974), p. 98.

But if we're honest, sometimes God's exorbitant grace aggravates us. We know this or that person—they don't deserve God's treasures. And those people over there—they certainly aren't worthy of them. How can God be so generous?

But then, if we think about it, we don't deserve God's favor either. All of us are equally needy—the heavy smoker, the alcoholic, the ex-con, the church member. We should not call any man unholy or unclean.

Remembering God's generosity toward us encourages our generosity toward others. Is there a Cornelius-type person in your life? How can you show that person God's lavish grace today?

_____

_____

_____

_____

_____

Chapter 3

GETTING OUT OF GOD'S WAY

Acts 11:1–18

God loves changing things. He moves His hand across the earth and the skies stir. He casts His shadow over a nation and a government topples. He whispers a word in the dark and a star fills the emptiness.

His favorite changes, though, occur in the hidden places, where the human soul and spirit mingle. He delights in changing a lonely boy's tears into laughter. He glories in converting a heart of stone into a heart of tenderness.

Yes, He loves His changes—the problem is that, too often, we resist them. He eagerly presses us to change and grow and move, but we keep stepping on the brakes.

Peter braked when God began altering his prejudice toward Gentiles. But he soon let up, and God carried him on to new avenues of grace. The Lord will do the same for us, but we must be open to change. The first step to such openness is an understanding of the nature of change.

Guiding Principles regarding Change

Initially, we must realize that *some changes are inevitable*. One ancient philosopher observed, "There is nothing permanent except change."[1] So, to stay up with our times, we must change with them. And to keep in step with God's plans for our times, we must let Him change us.

The second principle is that *any change requires adjustment*. Adjustments, though, are uncomfortable. It's awkward for parents to ask their children how to use the home computer. It's upsetting for organ-loving church members to get used to the new electric piano. Change tests our flexibility. It also tests our good judgment, for not all changes are necessarily positive.

---

1. Heraclitus, as quoted in *Peter's Quotations*, comp. Laurence J. Peter (New York, N.Y.: Bantam Books, 1977), p. 75.

That is the reason behind the third principle: *each change must be examined*. As we filter current trends through the Word of God, we discover which will help and which will hinder the communication of the gospel. But we must be careful to not confuse our ministry methods with God's truth, equating our preferences with Scripture and using our opinions as the grid.

Our goal, then, is to relevantly communicate the gospel to our society without altering God's truths. This requires an awareness of our times, spiritual wisdom, and a willingness to change—characteristics Peter found lacking in the early Jewish Christian leaders.

Facing Change in the First Century

Acts 10 concluded with Peter staying with Cornelius in Caesarea. The past few days had changed the Apostle forever. Christ had broken down the walls of prejudice separating the two men and joined them as Christian brothers.

This encounter also loosened the chains of legalism that still hung on Peter from his Jewish past. Now everything was clean in Christ, including Gentile food he previously would never have touched. We can imagine him sitting down for dinner with his new Gentile friends, staring at a plateful of pork. "In Christ, I'm free to eat this," he reassures himself, gulping down the surprisingly delicious nonkosher meal. God was changing Peter, and frankly, Peter was enjoying it.

Rigidity in Institutionalism

The time soon came for him to return home. But before he arrived in Jerusalem, the news of his association with Cornelius had already made the rounds.

> The apostles and the brethren who were throughout Judea heard that the Gentiles also had received the word of God. And when Peter came up to Jerusalem, those who were circumcised took issue with him, saying, "You went to uncircumcised men and ate with them." (11:1–3)

With the smell of ham still on his breath, Peter no sooner steps foot in the city before the Jewish Christians there begin pointing fingers and wagging tongues. "Shame on you, Peter!" "How could you, Peter?" "You've gone liberal, Peter!"

Institutional Judaism had begun rotting the church from the inside. Clinging to their past, Jewish believers supposed that being a good Christian also meant keeping the high standards of Jewish legalism. To them, the idea of a Christian Gentile was a contradiction in terms. And to think that Peter, their chief apostle, had not only been staying with Gentiles, but had been defiling himself by eating their food as well!

Account of Transformation

As he listens to their objections, Peter knows that the Jerusalem believers need to be transformed just as he has been. So,

> Peter began speaking and proceeded to explain to them in orderly sequence, saying, "I was in the city of Joppa praying; and in a trance I saw a vision, a certain object coming down like a great sheet lowered by four corners from the sky; and it came right down to me, and when I had fixed my gaze upon it and was observing it I saw the four-footed animals of the earth and the wild beasts and the crawling creatures and the birds of the air. And I also heard a voice saying to me, 'Arise, Peter; kill and eat.' But I said, 'By no means, Lord, for nothing unholy or unclean has ever entered my mouth.' But a voice from heaven answered a second time, 'What God has cleansed, no longer consider unholy.' And this happened three times, and everything was drawn back up into the sky." (vv. 4–10)

By relating his story to the people, Peter was building a bridge, so to speak, from his island of thinking to theirs. First, he simply stated the facts "in orderly sequence" rather than appealing to their emotions. Second, he showed them God's fingerprints all over his experience. Undeniably, God Himself designed not only the vision but also the events that followed it.

> "Behold, at that moment three men appeared before the house in which we were staying, having been sent to me from Caesarea. And the Spirit told me to go with them without misgivings. And these six brethren also went with me, and we entered the man's house. And he reported to us how he had seen

20

the angel standing in his house, and saying, 'Send to Joppa, and have Simon, who is also called Peter, brought here; and he shall speak words to you by which you will be saved, you and all your household.' And as I began to speak, the Holy Spirit fell upon them, just as He did upon us at the beginning. And I remembered the word of the Lord, how He used to say, 'John baptized with water, but you shall be baptized with the Holy Spirit.'" (vv. 11–16)

Issue of Fixation

Peter then reaches the pinnacle of his presentation:

"If God therefore gave to them the same gift as He gave to us also after believing in the Lord Jesus Christ, who was I that I could stand in God's way?" (v. 17)

He had walked the people over to the shore of change. Now they must decide whether to step off with Peter or turn their backs on God's way. If they refused the truth, they would have had what we might call a fixation—what *Webster's* defines as "an obsessive or unhealthy . . . attachment."[2] When confronted with change, we tend to fixate on the securities of the status quo. We cling to the rail of the bridge, fearful of anything new.

Peter had asked himself, "Who was I that I could stand in God's way?" And now he is asking the people the same question by implication: "Who are *you* to stand in God's way?" Would they loosen their grip on the past and accept God's new plan for the Gentiles?

Acceptance of Alteration

Luke records their response:

When they heard this, they quieted down, and glorified God, saying, "Well then, God has granted to the Gentiles also the repentance that leads to life." (v. 18)

Each one of them stepped off the bridge onto Peter's island and followed him into change. Once there, they gloried in God's marvelous grace—the grace that was bigger than any one of them could

2. *Webster's Ninth New Collegiate Dictionary,* see "fixation."

21

have imagined. The grace that would soon embrace the world with the splendor of Christ.

Applying Principles of Change Today

As we face change in our lives, let's draw inspiration from the early church's example. Recognizing the inevitability of change, let's be diligent, as were the Jerusalem Christians, to examine it in light of God's revelation and to accept its adjustments.

As we do, let's also keep in mind one other point: some things in Christianity are absolute and some are flexible. The Virgin Birth, Christ's sinlessness, His atonement, and other basics of our faith never fade, but the ways in which we express these truths can change.

So although our message is always the same, our method of communicating it must flex to meet the needs of our ever-changing world. As it does, we'll discover that God's ancient truths are as relevant today as when they were first written. Our Lord is forever on the cutting edge of our society; and that's where we can be, if we are open to change.

 Living Insights

Institutionalism can paralyze the muscles of any organization. Gene Getz describes its rigidifying effects in his book *Sharpening the Focus of the Church.* Although he recorded the following symptoms of institutionalism with the church in mind, see if they characterize parts of your world in some ways . . . perhaps your own church, or a parachurch organization you're part of, or even your own family.

Institutionalism occurs when:

1. The organization becomes more important than the people.

2. Individuals in the organization function more like cogs in a machine rather than vital parts of one another.

3. Individuality and creativity are lost.

4. The atmosphere of the organization is threatening rather than open and free. People are afraid to ask uncomfortable questions.

5. The structure has become rigid and inflexible.

6. People are serving the organization more than the original objectives of the organization. The means have become ends.

7. Communication often breaks down, frequently because of a repressive atmosphere.

8. People become prisoners of procedures. The rule book gets bigger and bigger.

9. In order to survive, people develop special interests and compete against each other. Unity is destroyed.

10. Morale degenerates, initiative erodes, and people become critical of the leaders.

11. A hierarchy of leadership develops, and people on the bottom feel as if they really don't count anymore.[3]

Do you see evidence of these symptoms in your world? Give some specific examples of the symptoms you've noticed.

_____

_____

_____

_____

The cure can begin with you. What symptoms of rigid institutionalism do you notice in your life? How can you experience God's grace to free your heart? How can you communicate that change to others?

_____

_____

_____

_____

3. Paraphrased from *Sharpening the Focus of the Church* by Gene A. Getz (Chicago, Ill.: Moody Press, 1974), pp. 193–94.

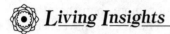

Peter returned from Caesarea floating on air. But as soon as he entered Jerusalem, the Christians there cocked their double-barreled rule book and immediately shot him down. Describe a time when others have shot you down for initiating a change.

_____

_____

_____

How can you increase the chances of people accepting your ideas the next time?

Initially, understand that an average of only 10 percent of the group are true inhibitors—the ones with the loaded rule books. Ten percent are innovators, those who are naturally open to change. And 80 percent are conservatives who simply require persuasion.[4] Therefore, target your ideas toward the majority—the conservatives who will vote for change if properly motivated.

To motivate the conservatives, communicate your suggested change in five stages. First, alert them to the need. People don't desire change until they are discontented with the status quo. Second, describe your goal, what you wish to accomplish. Third, outline how your changes will meet that goal. Fourth, guarantee the effectiveness of your changes with an evaluation plan, a way to measure and report progress.[5] Finally, realize that this simple plan will not fully motivate people unless they know that God is directing the change. This was the oil that loosened the resistant hearts in Peter's story.

You may be considering a change for your family, small group, or another area of ministry. If so, use the following space to outline how to communicate that change. And be sure to explain how God is in it.

The need: _____

_____

4. Getz, *Sharpening the Focus of the Church*, p. 256.

5. From Kenneth O. Gangel, *Feeding and Leading* (Wheaton, Ill.: Scripture Press Publications, Victor Books, 1989), pp. 151–52.

The goal: _____

_____

The plan: _____

_____

The evaluation proposal: _____

_____

How do you know that this change is God's will? _____

_____

_____

Chapter 4

OPERATION COMEBACK

Acts 11:19–30

A ncient Egypt is known for its pyramids, ancient Greece for its temples . . . and, interestingly, ancient Rome for its roads.

Roman roads once covered a total of 53,000 miles, extending through the outermost frontiers of the empire like so many arms from the mother city. They traversed wastelands, forded ravines, and crossed over mountains. They were engineering marvels— enduring reminders of Rome's passion to spread its empire throughout the world.

The book of Acts is also patterned with roads to the world— God's roads. But instead of stemming from Rome, His highways rolled out from Jerusalem, carrying the news of Christ to the earth's most distant corners.

This passion of God's for road building is revealed in the first chapter, where Jesus marked the construction plans for the early believers to follow.

> "You shall receive power when the Holy Spirit has come upon you; and you shall be My witnesses both in *Jerusalem, and in all Judea and Samaria, and even to the remotest part of the earth.*" (1:8, emphasis added)

The rest of Acts traces this blueprint. In chapters 1–7, the roads of witness are paved in Jerusalem; in chapters 8–12, they extend into Judea and Samaria; and in chapters 13–28, they course their ways through the far-flung enclaves of the ancient world. Today, though the writing of the book of Acts has ended, these roads are still expanding into new territory, as believers continue to clear more paths for the gospel's advance.

How exciting to realize that we can be as useful to God as those early believers! And what a privilege to stand in their company. Let's take a moment to review their contributions to the spread of God's kingdom and recall the lessons they've taught us.

Context: Men and Circumstances

Initially, God's chief engineer was Peter, who stood nose to nose with the Jewish leaders and relentlessly proclaimed the gospel throughout Jerusalem. However, for the message of Christ to progress beyond the Jews to the Gentiles, God had to bulldoze through boulders of prejudice in Peter and the other Jewish Christians.

Through Peter's encounter with Cornelius (10:1–11:18), God cleared away these roadblocks and widened the highway so all nationalities could come through. At the forefront of this new road, though, will be another leader. We've met him before; his name is Saul.

Saul had been the leading persecutor of the church, but he saw the light—literally—while traveling to Damascus and converted to Christianity (9:1–22). In Damascus, he became a vocal proponent for Christ and, after a few years, returned to Jerusalem with a fire in his soul for the gospel. The Jews, however, did not appreciate his newfound faith and switch in loyalties, and they plotted to kill him. So the Jerusalem Christians sent him back to his hometown, Tarsus, for his own safety (9:23–30). Although he didn't know it at the time, he would stay there, shelved and forgotten, for years.

With the Apostle to the Gentiles sequestered in Tarsus and the other Jewish Christians still a little reluctant to share the gospel beyond Jewish boundaries, how would God get His Word to the "remotest part of the earth"?

Persecution.

When Stephen was martyred, a great wave of persecution against Christians arose, which scattered believers into the regions of Judea and Samaria (8:1–4). The prelude to our lesson this time picks up on this theme.

> So then those who were scattered because of the persecution that arose in connection with Stephen made their way to Phoenicia and Cyprus and Antioch. (11:19a)

This scattering would actually be a turning point for Saul. For the persecution that propelled the gospel into Judea and Samaria had begun driving it along the Mediterranean coast to Phoenicia, then to the island of Cyprus, then as far north as Antioch, near Tarsus and Saul.

Outreach: Antioch and Evangelism

The persecuted believers who had traveled the three hundred miles from Jerusalem to Antioch carried with them the truth of

Christ. Wonderful! Except, initially, they were "speaking the word to no one except to Jews alone" (v. 19b). Unaware of the changes God had wrought through Peter's experience with Cornelius, these believers had bottled up the gospel and would only uncork it for "God's chosen." Thankfully, though, not all of the scattered Christians were so stingy with the new wine of Christ. Some of them were more forward-looking, trusting God to show them the new wineskins He would be poured into.

> But there were some of them, men of Cyprus and Cyrene,[1] who came to Antioch and began speaking to the Greeks also, preaching the Lord Jesus. (v. 20)

Barnabus and Saul in Antioch[2]

The result?

> The hand of the Lord was with them, and a large number who believed turned to the Lord. (v. 21)

Through these newborn multi-ethnic believers, God was unveiling His heart for the world. No longer would Jerusalem and the Jews be His only chosen ones; He would instead embrace all nations—which is symbolized in the shift to Antioch as the new hub of Christianity.

Assistance: Barnabas and Saul

The Jerusalem believers could have become jealous of Antioch as the rising star. But notice how they reacted:

> The news about them reached the ears of the church at Jerusalem, and they sent Barnabas off to Antioch. (v. 22)

1. Cyrene was located on the north African coast in what is Libya today.

2. *Life Application® Bible*, New International Version (copublishers; Wheaton, Ill: Tyndale House Publishers, 1991 and Grand Rapids, Mich.: Zondervan Publishing House, 1991), p. 1973. Maps © 1986, 1988 by Tyndale House Publishers, Inc. All rights reserved. Used by permission.

Saying, "Let's help them!" they sent their top man to them: Barnabas, the encourager.

Exhortation and Encouragement

When Barnabas arrived in Antioch and saw God's grace at work,

> he rejoiced and began to encourage them all with resolute heart to remain true to the Lord. (v. 23b)

How characteristic this was of Barnabas! Luke even stops to describe his outstanding qualities, calling him "a good man, and full of the Holy Spirit and of faith" (v. 24a). Like mortar, Barnabas cemented the bond between the churches and reinforced the commitment of the new Antioch believers. Because of his encouragement and hope, the church pulsated with enthusiasm, "and considerable numbers were brought to the Lord" (v. 24b).

Instruction and Identity

With the surge of new converts in Antioch, Barnabas humbly realized that the task was too big for him alone. So, remembering a certain bright and fiery man, he

> left for Tarsus to look for Saul; and when he had found him, he brought him to Antioch. (vv. 25–26a)

Saul's time had finally come. Probably arriving in Antioch like a whirlwind, he taught the people day in and day out (v. 26b). With Barnabas as his partner and mentor, Saul was making his comeback!

Despite their successes in the church, though, we should not think that ministering in Antioch was easy. Lloyd John Ogilvie comments:

> Syrian Antioch was a formidable place to begin a ministry. It was third only to Rome and Alexandria in prominence at the time. Known as one of the "eyes" of Asia, it was the residence of the Roman prefect and the seat of political power for that area of the Roman Empire. The culture of this metropolitan city at the mouth of the Orontes River was Greek. Strategically located fifteen miles from the Mediterranean Sea, Antioch had become very cosmopolitan. But something else had made the very name of the city synonymous with rampant immo-

rality. In this "sin city," chariot racing, gambling, and debauchery took priority in the persistent pursuit of pleasure. And controlling the ambience was the worship of Daphne, whose temple five miles out of the city housed prostitute priestesses. Apollo's famous pursuit of Daphne in the laurel groves around what became the site of the temple was reenacted night and day by the "worshipers" and the ritual prostitutes. The phrase "the morals of Daphne" became descriptive through the world of immorality at this time.[3]

Against this dark backdrop, the believers' Christlikeness became so obvious that their neighbors started calling them Christ-ians—partisans or followers of Christ. As Luke notes, "the disciples were first called Christians in Antioch" (v. 26c).[4]

What a fitting label for these devoted disciples of Jesus. In our day, the real meaning of the word *Christian* is almost lost in the fog of its familiarity. Let's not forget, though, the true meaning of our name. May our relationship to Christ be just as visible as that of the Antioch believers, so that people can comment to one another: "They must be Christ-ians."

Need: Jerusalem and Famine

The young church in Antioch not only reflected Christlike character to their own community, they demonstrated God's love to other believers as well. The opportunity came in the face of a natural disaster.

> Now at this time some prophets came down from Jerusalem to Antioch. And one of them named Agabus stood up and began to indicate by the Spirit that there would certainly be a great famine all over the world. And this took place in the reign of Claudius. (vv. 27–28)

3. Lloyd John Ogilvie, *Drumbeat of Love* (Waco, Tex.: Word Books, Publisher, 1976), pp. 152–53.

4. The name *Christian* is rarely used in the New Testament—once in Acts 26:28 and again in 1 Peter 4:16. It was given to the believers by the pagan community and probably had a slang usage at first.

Concerned about those needy believers in Judea, the Antioch Christians decided to help them . . . even before the need became a reality.

> And in the proportion that any of the disciples had means, each of them determined to send a contribution for the relief of the brethren living in Judea. And this they did, sending it in charge of Barnabas and Saul to the elders. (vv. 29–30)

The unselfishness of the Antioch believers was remarkable, especially considering that the most mature among them was only a few years old in the Lord. Through Barnabas and Saul's ministry, God was training them quickly. And through these young Gentile Christians' expression of love toward the Jewish church, the highway of God between the two peoples was completed. Barnabas and Saul traveled that road back to Jerusalem, triumphantly returning with the evidence of the gospel's power in people's lives.

Application for Today

As the partners journeyed back to Jerusalem, what was going through Saul's mind? Could he foresee the adventures that lay ahead of him, the countless roads he would travel for the sake of Christ? Did he realize the extent of his calling, the importance of his role as the one who would network the world with the highways of the gospel?

Saul's story reminds us that *whatever God pursues, He accomplishes* . . . and that *whomever God chooses, He uses.* And He may have chosen you to help build His roads and bridges to those whom He has yet to touch. It may not happen in your time frame; God may keep you on the side, waiting until the time is ripe, as He did with Saul. But whatever situation you may be in, you are on God's mind. And when your hour comes, no force in all the world will resist His power through you.

⊛ *Living Insights* STUDY ONE

Whatever God pursues, He accomplishes.

We know this to be true, yet how we wring our hands and pace and fret! Will the world crumble while His back is turned? Will a loved one's distress slip His notice? Will His plan for us, with all its good intentions, wither and blow away? Will His answer to our prayers get lost like a mislabeled letter in the mail?

Have you ever wondered, Can God really accomplish His purposes for me? If so, what areas of your life usually prompt this question?

_____

_____

_____

The story of Acts proves, if nothing else, that God can accomplish His purposes. Think of how God has spread His gospel throughout the world; and He began it all with just a few ordinary men and women like us.

Read the following verses, and write down how the truths contained in them restore your confidence in God's ability to accomplish whatever He intends in your life.

Job 42:2 _____

_____

Psalm 135:5–6 _____

_____

Ephesians 1:11 _____

_____

Philippians 1:6 _____

_____

⬡ *Living Insights* STUDY TWO

Whomever God chooses, He uses.

There is a corollary to this principle: Whomever God chooses, He uses . . . *but not always right away.* God chose Saul at his conversion. "He is a chosen instrument of Mine," God told Ananias, "to bear My name before the Gentiles and kings and the sons of Israel" (Acts 9:15). But the Lord didn't fully use Saul until years later, when Barnabas came looking for him in Tarsus.

Do you feel that God has chosen you for a special purpose but has left you waiting in a Tarsus? Are you struggling with this—anxious for Him to quit "stalling"? Reflect on any thoughts and feelings you are wrestling with.

_____

_____

_____

What do you think might be His purpose in this period of waiting?

_____

_____

_____

How can you use this time to prepare yourself so that when God calls your name, you will be ready?

_____

_____

_____

Chapter 5

MORE POWERFUL THAN PRISON BARS

Acts 12:1–17

$\mathbf{D}$ead end.

Few phrases convey as much hopelessness as this one. The word *end* is despairing enough, and then we preface it with the finality of the word *dead*. It makes us shudder!

Another word that is equally depressing is *impossibility*. Like a dead-end street, a dead-end job, or a dead-end relationship, an impossible situation has no visible solutions. There's no way around it, no way over it, and no way through it. The end is inevitable.

But whenever we view a problem as impossible, we are actually falling into a subtle trap—the trap of focusing on externals. Paul told the Corinthian believers, "You are looking at things as they are outwardly" (2 Cor. 10:7a), and we do the same thing by seeing only the wall and not the God of the wall. God is not limited like we are. He never faces dead ends. He doesn't even know what one looks like!

This fact prompted Paul to write,

> For though we walk in the flesh, we do not war
> according to the flesh, for the weapons of our warfare
> are not of the flesh, but divinely powerful for the
> destruction of fortresses. (vv. 3–4)

God provides divine weapons for us to use in our impossiblities. Let's observe some of these weapons in action in Acts 12, where we find Peter at his own dead-end street, sitting once again behind prison bars.

Initial Orientation

Since the stoning of Stephen nearly a decade before, a bleak winter of persecution had settled on the Jerusalem church, with no end in sight. When it seemed it could get no worse, another dark storm fell, blanketing the church in even more despair.

> Now about that time Herod the king laid hands
> on some who belonged to the church, in order to
> mistreat them. (v. 1)

Behind the thunderous threats and electric cruelty of torture was one man, the king of the Jews, Herod.

The name Herod was actually the man's surname, telling us that he was a member of Herod the Great's dynasty—a ruling family with close ties to the emperors in Rome. This Herod happened to be the grandson of Herod the Great, and Herod Agrippa I was his full name. He ruled Palestine from A.D. 37–44 as a puppet king under the Roman emperors Caligula and Claudius.

Like most of the Herods, Agrippa I ruled with one foot in Rome and the other in Jerusalem, as A. T. Robertson comments.

> Herod Agrippa I . . . was anxious to placate his
> Jewish subjects while retaining the favour of the Ro-
> mans. So he built theatres and held games for the
> Romans and Greeks and slew the Christians to
> please the Jews.[1]

In order to elevate his standing with the Jewish leaders, he had been cruelly tormenting believers, even to the point of murdering one of the apostles. "He had James the brother of John put to death with a sword" (v. 2).[2]

But his sadistic ploy for political favors did not stop there.

"When he saw that it pleased the Jews, he proceeded to arrest Peter also" (v. 3a).

Impossible Situation

Peter was next in line for the sword, but his execution had to wait because, as Luke reveals, he'd been arrested "during the days of Unleavened Bread"—the seven-day celebration that followed Passover (v. 3b). Because it was against the Jews' law to have a trial or execution during these holy days, Herod decided to

put him in prison, delivering him to four squads of

1. Archibald Thomas Robertson, *Word Pictures in the New Testament* (Grand Rapids, Mich.: Baker Book House, 1930), vol. 3, pp. 163–64.

2. Along with John and Peter, James had been a member of Jesus' inner circle. He was not the James who wrote the book of James. Rather, the author of that book was probably the brother of Jesus, whom Peter refers to in verse 17.

> soldiers to guard him, intending after the Passover
> to bring him out before the people. (v. 4)[3]

For Peter's friends, this situation looked impossible. First, this was Peter's third imprisonment (see Acts 4, 5). Second, he was absolutely surrounded. Four squads of four soldiers—two at the cell's door and the other two manacled to him—took turns guarding this "dangerous" prisoner (12:6c). Herod wasn't taking any chances of Peter mysteriously escaping his grasp (compare 5:17–20). And third, with the Feast of Unleavened Bread almost over, Peter's imprisonment would soon come to a deadly end. He was doomed. In fact, Luke says that it was "the very night when Herod was about to bring him forward" (12:6a).

There were no last-minute legal appeals to be made, no waiting rescue forces, no behind-the-scenes political maneuvering. From all outward appearances, the situation was impossible . . . and frightening. But was he trembling in anxiety's clutches? Not at all.

> Peter was sleeping between two soldiers, bound with
> two chains. (v. 6b)

Can you imagine sleeping while, down the hall, the executioner is sharpening the blade meant for you? Yet Peter trusted God, determined to glorify Him in life or death. Like Jesus, who slept while the waves crashed against His boat, Peter rested peacefully during his own storm. His faith in the Lord had made for a soft pillow.

And while Peter was trusting, his fellow believers were brandishing a divine weapon.

> Peter was kept in the prison, but prayer for him was
> being made fervently by the church to God. (v. 5)

The Greek tenses in this verse indicate that the Christians were continually and persistently praying. They were fighting a battle, not with fleshly instruments, but with weapons "divinely powerful for the destruction of fortresses" (see 2 Cor. 10:4).

The scene was set for a dramatic clash of two foes: physical might versus spiritual fervor. "Which will be the stronger," asks

---

3. "The 'Passover' here referred to the combined eight-day festival, the Passover itself followed by the seven days of unleavened bread." Stanley D. Toussaint, "Acts," in *The Bible Knowledge Commentary*, New Testament ed., ed. John F. Walvoord and Roy B. Zuck (Wheaton, Ill.: SP Publications, Victor Books, 1983), p. 384.

R. C. H. Lenski, "the dungeon and its guards or the prayers of the church?"[4]

Miraculous Intervention

The answer came that night while all was quiet.

Sudden Appearance

> Behold, an angel of the Lord suddenly appeared, and a light shone in the cell; and he struck Peter's side and roused him, saying, "Get up quickly." And his chains fell off his hands. (Acts 12:7)

At the darkest hour, God sent His angel of light. But Peter was sleeping so soundly, he didn't stir. The angel had to poke his ribs: "Wake up, Peter!"

> And the angel said to him, "Gird yourself and put on your sandals." And he did so. And he said to him, "Wrap your cloak around you and follow me." (v. 8)

Peter must have thought he was dreaming! On the floor were his chains, lying powerless next to the oblivious guards. In front of him was an angel, reminding him how to get dressed. He fumbled about and clothed himself, and still no one noticed him. Then he stumbled out of his cell after the angel. "If this *is* a dream, don't wake me!" Peter probably prayed.

Unexplainable Deliverance

> And when they had passed the first and second guard, they came to the iron gate that leads into the city, which opened for them by itself; and they went out and went along one street; and immediately the angel departed from him. (v. 10)

As Peter and the angel calmly walked by, the guards did not even stir. Then without a sound, God opened the iron gate, and Peter was free.

In our lives, there is not a lock that God can't pick. We may feel caged up in the past, in our own fears, or in destructive habits,

---

4. R. C. H. Lenski, *The Interpretation of the Acts of the Apostles* (Columbus, Ohio: Wartburg Press, 1944), p. 471.

but God is more powerful than any prison bars, real or internal. Nothing is impossible for Him.

Peter echoed this truth when he finally came to himself outside the prison gate.

> "Now I know for sure that the Lord has sent forth His angel and rescued me from the hand of Herod and from all that the Jewish people were expecting." (v. 11)

Natural Reaction

Peter made his way through the alleys and side streets "to the house of Mary, the mother of John who was also called Mark, where many were gathered together and were praying" (v. 12). Out of breath and flushed with excitement, he rapped on the door of the gate.

> A servant girl named Rhoda came to answer. And when she recognized Peter's voice, because of her joy she did not open the gate, but ran in and announced that Peter was standing in front of the gate. (vv. 13b–14)

"Peter is here!" said the wide-eyed girl to the others, not thinking that poor Peter would probably have liked to come in. "He's right at the gate and . . ."

"That's impossible!" the believers replied, perturbed that their prayers had been interrupted.

"But I heard him. I heard him!"

"Then you're hearing things. Now, where were we? Oh yes—'Mighty God, please deliver Peter from the hands . . .'"

"But I heard him!"

> And they said to her, "You are out of your mind!" But she kept insisting that it was so. And they kept saying, "It is his angel." (v. 15)

If Rhoda did hear a voice, maybe their fears had come true. "Could it be that they've killed Peter," wondered someone in the group, "and his angel has come to tell us?"[5]

---

5. This reference to Peter's angel is "probably an instance of the not uncommon belief that the moment a man dies his . . . angel appears. In this case, it would have been a sign that the Christians' prayer (cf. v. 5) had not been granted, but that Herod had had the apostle executed in prison." Johannes Munck, as quoted by Everett F. Harrison in *Interpreting Acts: The Expanding Church* (Grand Rapids, Mich.: Zondervan Publishing House, Academie Books, 1986), p. 204.

Everyone shivered at the thought—everyone except Rhoda.

"It is *Peter*, not some angel. Come to the door and . . . and . . . Oh my! I left him outside!"

Rhoda rushed to the door, with the group right behind her.

Meanwhile, Peter had been wondering whether he should try opening a window. But he

> continued knocking; and when they had opened the door, they saw him and were amazed. (v. 16)

"Peter? How . . . what? It *is* you!"

Pulling him quickly into the house, they enveloped him in a flurry of hugs and questions. Then,

> motioning to them with his hand to be silent, he described to them how the Lord had led him out of the prison. And he said, "Report these things to James and the brethren." And he departed and went to another place. (v. 17)

Peter left, instructing the believers to tell others about God's miracle in his life. In so doing, he shared the Light that opened his cell door.

Lessons for Today

That night, the believers in Jerusalem caught a glimpse of God's power to solve impossible problems. Their story reminds us of two principles that will keep our heads up when circumstances appear bleak.

First, *we are all faced with a series of great opportunities brilliantly disguised as impossible situations*. Everyone runs into his own wide, high, thick wall. Peter's wall even had bars, locks, and chains on it. From outward appearances, breaking that barrier was impossible; yet God unlocked Peter's cell, uncuffed his chains, and set him free. An impossible situation can turn into an opportunity for God to show His power.

Second, *if there is to be a solution, it will take divine intervention*. The group of praying believers were closed to the idea of God freeing Peter miraculously. We need to learn from their mistake—and remember that God can use a variety of ways, even miracles, to answer our prayers. He may use a person, a circumstance, or even a tragedy to amaze you with His supernatural power.

Whatever the situation you've written off as impossible, don't look at it outwardly. With your divinely powerful weapons of faith and prayer, turn your attitude, your habit, your circumstance over to Him. He'll take charge.

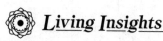 ## Living Insights

Are you locked up in an impossible situation? Your prison might be a difficult relationship, a frustrating job, an inner spiritual struggle, or anything that has you chained to a feeling of hopelessness. Write down what that might be.

_____

_____

_____

Viewing this situation outwardly, what aspects make it seem like an impossible problem to solve?

_____

_____

_____

If God broke the chains that bound Peter, He can break your chains as well. This is a proven fact. The question that remains is: How do we know that He will? After all, Peter was rescued, but James was not (Acts 12:2). Did Peter have more faith? Was the church praying harder for Peter?

Peter's rescue in contrast to James' death illustrates an important principle: We can't know whether God will perform a miracle in our lives, but we can still pray for one and trust Him with the results.

Modeling this principle for us are three men in the Old Testament who faced an impossibility: Shadrach, Meshach, and Abednego. They had refused to bow before King Nebuchadnezzar's golden image. Consequently, he was going to throw them into a blazing furnace. Apart from a miracle, it was impossible for them to survive the flames. What was their attitude during this impossible situation (Dan. 3:13–18)?

_____

_____

_____

God did intervene to save them (vv. 19–27); but even if He hadn't, they were determined to obey and glorify Him anyway. With this attitude and the divinely powerful weapons of faith and fervent prayer, no impossible situation can overwhelm us.

Use the following space to write down your words of trust in God's care, and commit yourself to doing the right thing, no matter what.

_____

_____

_____

_____

🏵 *Living Insights* STUDY TWO

C. H. Spurgeon imagined prayer this way:

> You see the men in the belfry sometimes down below with the ropes. They pull them, and if you have no ears, that is all you know about it. But the bells are ringing up there. They are talking and discoursing sweet music up aloft in the tower. And our prayers do, as it were, ring the bells of heaven.[6]

How would you characterize the ringing of your prayers lately?

___ Like clock-tower bells, regular and strong.
___ Like church bells, heard only on Sundays.
___ Like dinner bells, short and routine.
___ Like doorbells, small and polite.
___ Like service bells, loud and demanding.

6. C. H. Spurgeon, *Spurgeon at His Best*, comp. Tom Carter (Grand Rapids, Mich.: Baker Book House, 1988), p. 146.

___ Like glass bells, hollow and showy.
___ Like alarm bells, ear-splitting and panicky.

For our prayers to be most effective, they must be regular and strong, like clock-tower bells. The Christians in our story, despite their weak faith, offered clock-tower prayers on Peter's behalf. What characteristics of their prayers made them effective (see Acts 12:5, 12)?

_____

_____

If your prayers seem to be like a weak tinkling in God's ears, what do you think is causing the problem? Possibly a secret sin (see Ps. 66:18)? A hidden grudge (see Matt. 5:23–24)? Write down what could be weakening your prayers.

_____

_____

_____

Strengthening your prayers may require a new method in praying. The following are two suggestions. If you have any further ideas for building up your prayers, list them in the space provided. Pick a method and start ringing the bells of heaven today.

• Make a prayer journal, listing your requests on one half of the page and the answers on the other half.

• Fold a piece of paper into six sections. Label each section with six days of the week—Monday through Saturday. Write down a few different prayer requests for each day in the sections. Then on Sunday, review the lists, note which requests were answered, and prepare another sheet for the next week.

Your ideas: _____

_____

_____

Chapter 6

CONTRASTING LIFESTYLES

Acts 12:18–25

A mid the churning waters of the San Francisco Bay, an island of solid rock stands fast against its tumultuous surroundings. This island is Alcatraz, once the site of the most secure federal penitentiary in the United States. "After it became a maximum security federal prison in 1934,

> no convict was known to have lived to tell of a
> successful escape from the prison of Alcatraz Island.
> . . . A total of 23 men attempted it but 12 were
> recaptured, five shot dead, one drowned and five
> presumed drowned.[1]

The prisoners sentenced to Alcatraz knew there was no hope of escape. Peter must have felt like one of those inmates when Herod threw him behind bars. Locked up in the dark recesses of a Roman prison, Peter was shackled to two soldiers and watched by two more guards at the door. It would take a miracle to escape this prison. And that's exactly what happened.

The night before Peter's perfunctory trial and execution, an angel led him right past the guards to freedom. Not until the next morning was the alarm sounded—but by then it was too late. Peter was gone, and the soldiers were left to inform Herod that his prize prisoner had vanished.

Opposing Viewpoints

As we examine the events following Peter's escape, we will notice two opposing viewpoints: the non-Christian and the Christian. The non-Christian guards must have agonized among themselves over what to say to Herod. A Roman soldier didn't believe in miracles—but what other explanation was there?

Peter, on the other hand, had no trouble acknowledging the miracle he explained to his waiting friends.

---

1. Donald McFarlan, ed., *The Guinness Book of Records 1991* (New York, N.Y.: Facts on File, 1990), p. 218.

For the Christian

Peter had made his way to Mary's house, and there "he described to them how the Lord had led him out of the prison" (Acts 12:17). His statement reflected the perspective of a Christian: God had unshackled his chains; God had kept the guards from noticing him; God had opened the prison gates. These things didn't happen by chance.

We sometimes forget that God is behind the events in our lives. We'll say without thinking, "Luckily, I got the job." Or, "The car just happened to swerve away from my child." But these kinds of blessings don't shine on us by chance. God is sovereign; He's in control of our good and bad circumstances. It is the non-Christian who believes in luck—something that, from the guards' point of view, turned bad when, the next morning, they saw they were chained to thin air.

For the Non-Christian

> Now when day came, there was no small distur-
> bance among the soldiers as to what could have
> become of Peter. (v. 18)

Literally, the phrase reads, "there was a disturbance, not a small one." The word *disturbance* here means "trouble" or "tumult." The realization of Peter's escape stirred up the guards like a rock thrown in a pond of sleeping fish. Wide-eyed and frantic over what had happened, the soldiers raced this way and that looking for Peter.

By their actions, they betrayed their point of view. Because they couldn't admit that God had supernaturally rescued Peter, they had to search for a rational explanation for the escape. This thinking illustrates a fundamental difference between Christians and non-Christians: non-Christians cannot comprehend the work of God when it defies empirical reasoning.[2]

Different Reactions

The believers had contended, "The Lord led Peter out." But the guards were saying, "He's got to be around here somewhere; let's

---

2. For example, the Jewish leaders couldn't accept Jesus' resurrection miracle, so they paid the guards at the tomb to say that thieves stole the body (Matt. 28:11–15). Some non-Christians today are still using that argument to explain away the resurrection.

look for him." The miracle became a watershed, forcing the believers toward greater faith and the unbelievers toward greater despair. Let's follow the unbelievers in the story first, noting their reactions to Peter's miraculous escape in the hours and days that followed.

Among Unbelievers

Initially, the guards felt *confusion*. This led to panic, then panic led to bewilderment. Peter was nowhere to be found! Where could he be? What had happened? How had the chains fallen off? The guards certainly couldn't find any answers to their questions, and neither could Herod when he arrived on the scene.

Herod exhibited just as much confusion as the guards, but his reaction went one step further. His bewilderment led to suspicion.

> When Herod had searched for him and had not found him, he examined the guards. (v. 19a)

The word *examined* can imply interrogation by torture. Herod was going to grill a confession out of these soldiers, because for him, only one explanation seemed plausible: conspiracy.

Herod's suspicions were wrong, however; and though he tried to settle the matter through blaming the guards, his reaction spiraled further downward into *frustration*. Like a child who can't get his way, Herod let his frustration erupt into uncontrollable anger: "He examined the guards and ordered that they be led away to execution" (v. 19b).

Then he tried to escape from the whole bothersome situation: "He went down from Judea to Caesarea and was spending time there" (v. 19b).

Escapism is a natural response for those who cannot turn to the Lord. Some may flee into drugs or alcohol; others may run to the embrace of an illicit affair. But they're only deceiving themselves when they think they can outrun their problems. And Herod was no exception.

Bringing his own sinful anger and pride right along with him, Herod became a seething volcano—showering the hapless people of Tyre and Sidon with his molten wrath.

> Now he was very angry with the people of Tyre
> and Sidon; and with one accord they came to him,
> and having won over Blastus the king's chamberlain,
> they were asking for peace, because their country

was fed by the king's country. (v. 20)

Through cunning political maneuvering, the people pleaded through Blastus for peace with the king. And on an appointed day, Herod planned to answer their request. But he made one fatal mistake. He mounted the platform of *self-exaltation.*

> And on an appointed day Herod, having put on his royal apparel, took his seat on the rostrum and began delivering an address to them. And the people kept crying out, "The voice of a god and not of a man!" (vv. 21–22)

The ancient Jewish historian Josephus elaborates on this foreboding scene.

> He put on a garment made wholly of silver, and of a contexture truly wonderful, and came into the theatre early in the morning; at which time the silver of his garment being illuminated by the fresh reflection of the sun's rays upon it, shone out after a surprising manner, and was so resplendent as to spread a horror over those that looked intently upon him: and presently his flatterers cried out, one from one place, and another from another . . . that he was a god.[3]

Caught up in his moment of glory, Herod did the unthinkable: he accepted the blasphemous praise.

> And immediately an angel of the Lord struck him because he did not give God the glory, and he was eaten by worms and died. (v. 23)

What a horrible death! Yet what a poignant illustration of many people today, particularly celebrities, who thrive on fame and power. Like Herod, those who crave human praise often become victims of it, consumed by their own pride.

Death was the ultimate end for Herod, who vehemently opposed God. But the Christians' path, although unnoticed by the crowds, led to another end.

---

3. William Whiston, trans., *Josephus: Complete Works* (1960; reprint, Grand Rapids, Mich.: Kregel Publications, 1978), p. 412.

Among Believers

After Peter's miraculous rescue, the faith and the witness of the Christians flourished.

> But the word of the Lord continued to grow and to be multiplied.
> And Barnabas and Saul returned from Jerusalem when they had fulfilled their mission, taking along with them John, who was also called Mark. (vv. 24–25)

Notice the positive tone in these verses. In spite of Herod's threats, the gospel was spreading. Although it was a time of testing in Jerusalem, Barnabas and Saul fulfilled their mission of delivering aid to the church (see 11:29–30). And even though the circumstances remained bleak, the two elder apostles had the vision to encourage and train young John Mark.

The world may have been preoccupied with Herod and his pretentious splendor, but God's hand was working mightily behind the scenes. Like a countermelody, the gospel was playing on, and soon the world would take notice of its soft but pleasant strain.

Application for Today

In this passage, we've seen two contrasting perspectives and two ultimate ends. The Christian path led to hope and growth; the non-Christian road led to frustration and death. As we stand at the crossroads of these two ways, let's look at two signposts of advice that the Scripture has left for us.

First, *to make any deep change in life, we need the help of God.* When exaltation comes our way, He can help us change our pride into humility. He can change our weaknesses into strengths and our frustrations into victories. It may not be easy, but with His help anything is possible.

Second, *once we've tasted of Christ's provision, nothing else satisfies.* The peace that comforted Peter, the wonder of seeing a miracle, and the thrill of answered prayer are blessings that nonbelievers have never tasted. Once they do, however, nothing else satisfies. Journalist Malcolm Muggeridge decided to hold the cup of Christ to his lips one day. What he discovered can be your experience as well, when you drink from Christ's limitless supply.

I may, I suppose, regard myself, or pass for being, a relatively successful man. People occasionally stare at me in the streets—that's fame. I can fairly easily earn enough to qualify for admission to the higher slopes of the Internal Revenue—that's success. Furnished with money and a little fame even the elderly, if they care to, may partake of trendy diversions—that's pleasure. It might happen once in a while that something I said or wrote was sufficiently heeded for me to persuade myself that it represented a serious impact on our time—that's fulfillment. Yet I say to you—and I beg you to believe me—multiply these tiny triumphs by a million, add them all together, and they are nothing—less than nothing, a positive impediment—measured against one draught of that living water Christ offers to the spiritually thirsty, irrespective of who or what they are.[4]

 Living Insights

A Christian can act like a non-Christian, just like a free man can act like a slave. But why would we want to? The motivator is our flesh, which prompts us to become more like Herod, the unbeliever, and less like Peter, the believer. Take the following true-false quiz to determine whose perspective you've been imitating lately.

Herod's Perspective

_____ Recently, I've been using the words *luck* and *by chance* a lot.

_____ When others say that God performed a miracle, I usually discount it as a coincidence or a result of natural causes.

_____ When I encounter an unsolvable problem, I often panic and even look for someone to blame.

_____ Lately I've resembled a rumbling volcano, erupting angrily at any provocation.

4. Malcolm Muggeridge, *Jesus Rediscovered* (Garden City, N.Y.: Doubleday and Co., 1969), p. 61.

___ I often think of how to gain more power and fame; and when others praise me, I take all the credit.

Peter's Perspective

___ I have been acknowledging God's hand in everything that happens to me.

___ I've felt the joy of discovering miracles, even in the everyday events of my life.

___ When faced with an impossibility, I trust the Lord.

___ When in frustrating circumstances, I patiently wait for God's hand.

___ If others praise me, I thank them but give the glory to God.

Which category had the greatest number of *true* responses? If your perspective has been more like unbelieving Herod's, how can you change your point of view to that of Peter the believer?

Take a moment to read another apostle's advice for doing this, in Colossians 3:1–17. Write down all of Paul's commands in these verses.

_____

_____

_____

_____

_____

_____

What is our foundation for being able to follow these commands (see especially vv. 1, 3–4, 10, 12–13)?

_____

_____

_____

Our position in Christ gives us our Christian perspective. With His strength, we can avoid Herod's dead-end road and stay on Peter's path toward life and peace.

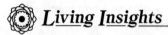

Imagine that all the people in the world were members of a huge orchestra. The first violinists would be those people in the headlines, the ones whose faces are on all the magazine covers. While the other instruments follow along, they would be playing the main melody—a melody of living for pleasure, striving for material gain, longing for recognition.

However, also imagine a lone oboist or flutist playing a counter-melody. One against many, yet that one subtle strain pierces through the rest.

As Christians, we are the ones playing the countermelody. Sometimes, though, we yearn to abandon our part and follow the more dominant theme. Have you been playing the world's tune lately? If so, in what ways?

God created you to play a different part. It may not shake the auditorium or rouse the critics, but it will please the Composer. That countermelody is the teaching of Jesus—loving God, loving your neighbor, praying for your enemies. In what ways, this week, can you play your part more clearly?

Chapter 7

HOW GOD
MOVES PEOPLE

Acts 13:1–4a

For many people, Willie Nelson's song "On the Road Again" is
more than just a fun car-trip sing-along. It's a way of life.

Moving from city to city, job to job, school to school these days
has become commonplace. Just consider your own neighborhood.
How many people have you seen move in or out lately?

And what about you? How many times have you moved during
the past few years?

Although few of us enjoy moving, when a higher standard of
living or a chance for a cozier neighborhood comes knocking on
the door, off we go—on the road again. For the Christian, though,
there is another reason for moving: God. When He says it's time
to go, although we may not understand why, we set out, like Abraham, to a land we do not know.

The book of Acts is a log of that kind of traveling. People are
on the move, setting off in one direction or another in response to
God's call. This lesson brings us to one such launching point when
God clearly said it was time to move.

Behind the Scenes: A Plan

Remember God's plan in Acts 1:8? "You shall be My witnesses
. . . in Jerusalem."

Jerusalem was as far as His witnesses went, until the stones of
persecution hit the calm waters and sent the Christians rippling
outward into the second phase of God's plan—Judea and Samaria.
Once having put down some roots there, though, could it be that
they had forgotten the last part of Jesus' instructions: "And even to
the remotest part of the earth" (v. 8b)?

Certainly, we can understand their desire to stay settled, their
need for security. But when God has a plan, He knows what He is
doing. And this is just as true for transplanted Christians now as it
was in the first century.

God's plan to get these Christians on the road again is the
subject of this passage. Let's go to Acts 13 and see how the Holy

Spirit will move His people into a new territory . . . one we are still exploring today.[1]

Making the Move: A Need

The first few words of Acts 13:1 provide a backdrop for the action that follows.

> Now there were at Antioch, in the church that was there, prophets and teachers.

Current Situation

Though his phrasing is simple, Luke conveys a wealth of information in his portrait of the situation. First, he mentions Antioch—the Roman capital of Syria and the gateway to the east. Like most large cities, Antioch was multicultural, trade-rich, and bawdy. On the outskirts of town stood the temple of Daphne, a deplorable center of prostitution and pagan worship. Chariot racing and sports lured gamblers into the city, where the atmosphere exuded a high-rolling style.

In distinct contrast to the city, another image emerges on Luke's canvas: the church. Under the glaring lights of the big city, the Lord was kindling the warm flame of Christian faith and morality. That is His way. Where the need is greatest, the Lord will be working, establishing His church as a beachhead against the forces of Satan.

A closer look at verse 1—"Now there were . . . prophets and teachers"—reveals the ministry at the church. Everett Harrison helps us distinguish these two ministries.

> As a prophet, a person spoke in response to a distinct moving of the Spirit, providing edification, exhortation, and consolation (1 Cor. 14:3). As a teacher, one presumably had a more sustained ministry, making use of the Old Testament and the traditions of the life and teaching of the Lord Jesus as handed down in the church (Acts 2:42; cf. Matt. 28:20). The teacher provided the basic information

---

1. Acts 13 begins the third main division in the book. The church was *established* in Jerusalem (chaps. 1–7), *scattered* to Judea and Samaria (chaps. 8–12), and now, through the rest of Acts, it will *extend* to the remotest parts of the earth.

for living the Christian life; the prophet furnished special guidance from the Lord as needed.[2]

These prophets and teachers included five men:

> Barnabas, and Simeon who was called Niger, and Lucius of Cyrene, and Manaen who had been brought up with Herod the tetrarch, and Saul. (v. 1b)

It's easy to skip over a verse like this, thinking that it's just another list of difficult-to-pronounce names. But we'd miss a significant insight if we did, for these leaders reflect a great diversity of backgrounds. Barnabas was from the island of Cyprus. Simeon also had the name Niger, which, according to Harrison, was "a Latin term meaning 'black-skinned.'"[3] Lucius was from Cyrene, which was west of Egypt on the coast of Africa. His name was Greek, so he was possibly a Gentile. Manaen was a member of high society, having grown up with Herod Antipas, the ruler of Galilee and Perea.[4] And then there's Saul with his impressive education and rabbinical training.

A Cyprian Jew, a black man, a Gentile, an aristocrat, and a rabbi—this was a cosmopolitan leadership team! With such backgrounds, they were better able to minister to the many ethnic groups in Antioch. Consequently, the church body had become a model of diversity within unity—a microcosm of God's upcoming worldwide, multicultural ministry.

Divine Interruption

To launch this worldwide program, the Holy Spirit interrupts the church's thriving ministry with a sudden command.

> And while they were ministering to the Lord and fasting, the Holy Spirit said, "Set apart for Me Barnabas and Saul for the work to which I have called them." (v. 2)

Notice, first, the Holy Spirit spoke "while they were ministering."

---

2. Everett F. Harrison, *Interpreting Acts: The Expanding Church* (Grand Rapids, Mich.: Zondervan Publishing House, Academie Books, 1986), p. 214.

3. Harrison, *Interpreting Acts*, p. 215.

4. The Greek word translated "brought up with" can mean "foster brother." Manaen and Herod Antipas may not have only been playmates as boys, but members of the same family. See Harrison, *Interpreting Acts*, p. 215.

We don't always need to escape to a mountaintop to sense God's leading. Often the best time to hear His voice is while we're busy reaching out to others, counseling, or sharing the gospel. We're most sensitive at these times because the Spirit is already empowering us for ministry. It's a ripe moment for Him to lean over and whisper a word in our ears.

We don't know exactly how the Holy Spirit led the congregation to set apart the two leaders for missions, but we do know that His plan was selective and specific. The call wasn't for everyone, just Barnabas and Saul. And they weren't to choose their own field; God had a specific work for them to do.

The fact that God's calling is selective and specific is encouraging, because it reaffirms how personal His map is for each of our paths. So we needn't feel guilty when He guides our friends in one direction—college or marriage or missions—and does not lead us that same way.

Ideal Transition

Barnabas and Saul obey God right away. The future may be a mystery to them, but they trust His new direction for their lives. The assembly of believers in Antioch trust God too, by supporting the men's transition from church leaders to missionaries.

> When they had fasted and prayed and laid their hands on them, they sent them away. (v. 3)

This affirmation of Barnabas and Saul was a sign of the church's maturity. They didn't cling to their friends but released them, knowing that God's will was best. God would take up the slack in leadership with other gifted teachers and prophets.

The people give Barnabas and Saul their blessing, but the Holy Spirit gives them His authority. Verse 4 begins, "Being sent out by the Holy Spirit . . ." His plan to reach the remotest part is set in motion, and with great anticipation, the missionaries launch out to hand deliver the good news of Christ. Having been enthusiastically set to sea by their fellow Christians, they unfurl their sails in the wind of God's Spirit as Antioch fades in the distance.

Following the Lord: An Application

Following the Lord is an adventure. It is a courageous voyage to lands only He knows. Are you willing to climb aboard and let

Him send you where He wills? If you are, keep these four principles handy as you wait for His call.

First, *do not automatically remove any possibility.* God may be pointing you toward something new—a new ministry, a new location, or a new friendship. So be open to the Spirit's quiet prompting, and don't limit His potential through you. Second, *don't allow activity to dull your senses.* Be careful not to let even worthy church involvement distract you from hearing God's new course for your life. Third, *remember: God's moves are always selective.* Be careful not to judge others who stay behind or to feel guilty because God chose someone else. And fourth, *when God says, "Go"*—obey. Let the Lord take the helm in your life and in the lives of those you love. The seas may be rough, the heading unknown, but there is no safer place to be than under His flag.

 Living Insights

Change means stress.

Thomas Holmes and Richard Rahe measured the amount of change-related stress on a scale of what they called life-change units.[5] The higher the number of units you accumulate in one year, the greater will be your stress as well as the chances of stress-related illness. The following excerpt from their rating scale reveals the number of life-change units associated with a typical household's move. According to Holmes and Rahe, a score of 300 or above indicates a high likelihood of stress-related health problems.

Business readjustment	39
Change in financial state	38
Mortgage over $10,000	31
Change in responsibilities at work	29
Wife begins or stops work	26
Change in living conditions	25
Change in work hours or conditions	20
Change in residence	20
Change in schools	20
Change in recreation	19
Change in church activities	19

5. Thomas H. Holmes, Richard H. Rahe, "Social Readjustment Rating Scale," in *Encyclopedia of Psychology* (n.p., 1984).

Change in social activities   18
Change in number of family get-togethers   15

Altogether, the changes involved in a move total 319 life-change units. Add this to other events of your life, such as divorce, personal injury, retirement, or death of a close friend, and your number of life-change units would soar sky-high—along with your blood pressure!

As Saul and Barnabas moved into the unknown, their faith in God's sovereignty gave them shelter in the storms of stress. If you're in the process of a move or a significant change, how can your faith in the Lord protect your emotional and physical well-being?

_____

_____

_____

_____

Take a few moments to memorize the following verses as you venture into your unknown. Let the Lord give you the stability you need during the changes in your life.

"Blessed is the man who trusts in the Lord
And whose trust is the Lord.
For he will be like a tree planted by the water,
That extends its roots by a stream
And will not fear when the heat comes;
But its leaves will be green,
And it will not be anxious in a year of drought
Nor cease to yield fruit." (Jer. 17:7–8)

Living Insights   STUDY TWO

In his book *The Sacred Journey*, Frederick Buechner describes the meaning he found in the simplicity of a rainy day.

> I loved the rain as a child. I loved the sound of
> it on the leaves of trees and roofs and window panes
> and umbrellas and the feel of it on my face and bare
> legs. I loved the hiss of rubber tires on rainy streets

and the flip-flop of windshield wipers. I loved the smell of wet grass and raincoats and the shaggy coats of dogs. A rainy day was a special day for me in a sense that no other kind of day was—a day when the ordinariness of things was suspended with ragged skies drifting to the color of pearl and dark streets turning to dark rivers of reflected light and even people transformed somehow as the rain drew them closer by giving them something to think about together, to take common shelter from, to complain of and joke about in ways that made them more like friends than it seemed to me they were on ordinary sunny days. But more than anything, I think, I loved rain for the power it had to make indoors seem snugger and safer and a place to find refuge in from everything outdoors that was un-home, unsafe.[6]

When God interrupts our routines and moves us, it can seem like a rainy day—uncertain, foreboding, dark. But the One who showers us with change also huddles us together in the home of His presence. So like the rain, change has the power to make God "seem snugger and safer and a place to find refuge in."

Look up the following verses, and write down the variety of rainy-day circumstances within which God gives us refuge.

Psalm 7:1 _____

Psalm 46:1–3 _____

Isaiah 25:4 _____

From these next verses, write down ways you can respond to God's refuge.

Psalm 59:16–17 _____

Psalm 62:5–8 _____

Psalm 73:28 _____

As sure as God sends rain, He will from time to time cloud your horizon with change. So seek His refuge, and let it pour!

6. Frederick Buechner, *The Sacred Journey* (San Francisco, Calif.: Harper and Row, Publishers, 1982), pp. 18–19.

Chapter 8

REACHING THE
REMOTEST PART

Survey of Acts 13:4–21:17

Tomorrow your journey begins. All the "to-dos" on your list have been done. Your bags are packed and at the front door. The timers on the lights have been set. Now quietness blankets the house, disturbed only by the hall clock chiming midnight. And you lay in bed . . . wide awake with worry.

"Did we buy enough traveler's checks? Will our car make the trip? The weather report forecasts storms—what if the roads close? Remember to put blankets in the trunk. What if the kids catch the flu? I think I'm catching the flu. I knew we should have postponed this trip!"

Pre-vacation goblins haunt all of us the night before a trip. Imagine, though, Saul's trepidations before his journeys. The book of Acts records four of his extended voyages: three missionary ventures and a final one-way trip to Rome. These were not vacation jaunts but perilous expeditions. At every turn, Saul faced

> dangers from rivers, dangers from robbers, dangers
> from my countrymen, dangers from the Gentiles,
> dangers in the city, dangers in the wilderness, dan-
> gers on the sea, dangers among false brethren.
> (2 Cor. 11:26)

Before his trips, did Saul lay wide awake with worry? Did he long to postpone his plans?

We can be thankful that, whatever fears he might have had, he still had the courage to leave the familiar and venture out into the unknown. Wherever the Holy Spirit told him to go, he went. As a result, the flame of Christ spread to the Asians, then to the Europeans, and eventually down through time to us. All because he let God direct his steps.

Acts 13:4–21:17 focuses on Saul's three missionary journeys, which we will survey in this lesson.[1] As we grab our bags and trail

---

1. The first missionary journey is found in Acts 13:4–14:28; the second, Acts 15:36–18:22; and the third, Acts 18:23–21:17.

along behind, let's remember the debt we owe him for bringing the gospel to our distant ancestors, those who lived in the remotest part of the earth.

Comments about the Survey

When Barnabas and Saul weighed anchor and set sail on their first missionary journey, God must have thrown a terrific bon voyage party in heaven. This was a horn-blowing, confetti-throwing occasion. He longed for the whole world to know His Son.

Jesus Himself had voiced this driving passion when He said, "Go therefore and make disciples of all the nations" (Matt. 28:19a) and, "Preach the gospel to all creation" (Mark 16:15b). Even His very last words were, "You shall be My witnesses . . . even to the remotest part of the earth" (Acts 1:8).

Within these final instructions to His disciples, Jesus emphasized His strategy to reach the world. First, *people* would proclaim His message, rather than voices from heaven or angels or miraculous skywriting. Second, His approach would be *simple:* start where you are and go out from there. Third, His method would be *personal*. He didn't want a Madison Avenue advertising campaign, just one life touching another with His love.

Charting Out the Journeys

Saul carried out Christ's strategy in his missionary journeys, the first of which began from Antioch in Syria. Let's follow him in his adventures as Christ's witness to the world.

The First Missionary Journey

Traveling with Barnabas and young John Mark, Saul sets off to the island of Cyprus, Barnabas' homeland. Their ship lands at Salamis, and from there, they trek across to Paphos, preaching the gospel from place to place. During this time, Saul's name changes to Paul (13:9), and an important city official believes in Christ (v. 12).

Feeling confident about their first-round success, they sail to what is now southern Turkey. Here Paul possibly contracts malaria—perhaps the source of a lingering "bodily illness" or eye disease (Gal. 4:13–14). And the frightened and homesick John Mark abandons the mission and goes home (Acts 13:13).

Paul and Barnabas press on without him, though, going up to

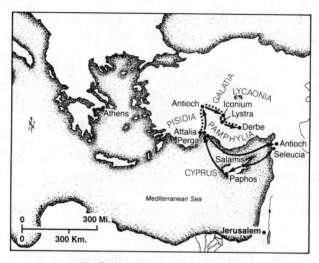

Paul's First Missionary Journey[2]

Pisidian Antioch. Paul preaches in the synagogue, and the "whole city assembled to hear the word of God" (v. 44b). The Gentiles embrace the gospel message, but the Jews

> instigated a persecution against Paul and Barnabas, and drove them out of their district. (v. 50b)

In spite of this, the two missionaries are "continually filled with joy and with the Holy Spirit" (v. 52b); so they hike on to Iconium—but the people there try to stone them. Narrowly escaping the violence in this city, they flee to Lystra, where tragedy strikes. The people "stoned Paul and dragged him out of the city, supposing him to be dead" (14:19b).

Tossed out of the city like a dead animal, Paul lies motionless in the dirt as a group of sympathetic disciples gather around him. Miraculously, his eyes move slightly, then his arms; then, with amazing courage, "he arose and entered the city" (v. 20). God can't let Paul die now—there are people who need to hear the gospel!

The next day he leaves with Barnabas for Derbe. Then the two men retrace their steps, encouraging the new believers in Lystra,

2. *Life Application® Bible*, New International Version (copublishers; Wheaton, Ill.: Tyndale House Publishers, 1991 and Grand Rapids, Mich.: Zondervan Publishing House, 1991), p. 1988. Maps © 1986, 1988 by Tyndale House Publishers, Inc. All rights reserved. Used by permission.

Iconium, Pisidian Antioch, and Perga. They conclude their journey by sailing back to Antioch in Syria; and when they arrive home, they report

> all things that God had done with them and how He had opened a door of faith to the Gentiles. And they spent a long time with the disciples. (vv. 27b–28)

The Second Missionary Journey

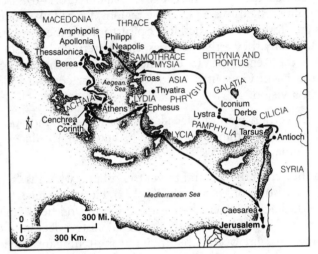

Paul's Second Missionary Journey[3]

Before carrying the gospel to even more distant regions, Paul briefly travels to Jerusalem with Barnabas to help resolve a doctrinal clash. Does a Gentile need to be circumcised and follow the Mosaic Law in order to be saved? A council of apostles and elders forms, and they concur: salvation is available to all who believe (15:1–29). Paul and Barnabas return to Antioch and determine to make a second missionary journey. But before they can go, another clash occurs—this time between two good friends.

Barnabas wants to give John Mark another chance, but Paul refuses to take him along.

> And there arose such a sharp disagreement that they

3. *Life Application® Bible*, p. 1988. Maps © 1986, 1988 by Tyndale House Publishers, Inc. All rights reserved. Used by permission.

separated from one another, and Barnabas took Mark
with him and sailed away to Cyprus. But Paul chose
Silas and departed. (vv. 39–40a)

So Paul, with his new partner Silas, journeys overland through
the Cilician Gates, across the perilous Taurus Mountains. They
encourage the Christians in Derbe, Lystra—where they pick up
Timothy—Iconium, and other cities. Then on they move to more
unevangelized areas in Phrygia and Galatia (16:1–6). But God
doesn't allow them to stay in these regions, for as Luke comments,
they were "forbidden by the Holy Spirit to speak the word in Asia"
(v. 6b). Finally they arrive at Troas, the western end of Asia on the
shores of the Aegean Sea (v. 8), where Luke joins the team. Should
they turn back? Go south? North? The answer comes to Paul one
night in a vision:

A certain man of Macedonia was standing and appealing to him, and saying, "Come over to Macedonia and help us." (v. 9)

So they cross the sea and travel to Philippi, which is "a leading
city of the district of Macedonia" (v. 12a). Here they meet a devout
woman, Lydia, who opens her heart to Christ and her home to all
of them (vv. 14–15). Not long after, Paul casts a demon out of an
exploited slave girl. Seeing that their fortune-telling income is gone,
her masters angrily have Paul and Silas beaten and thrown in jail
(vv. 16–23). Undaunted, Paul and Silas sing praises to God, and

suddenly there came a great earthquake, so that the
foundations of the prison house were shaken; and
immediately all the doors were opened, and everyone's chains were unfastened. (v. 26)

A frightened jailer sees all the open doors and draws a sword to
kill himself. But Paul calls out to stop him, reassuring him that all
the prisoners are still there. He is so impressed with their Christianity that he asks, "Sirs, what must I do to be saved?" (v. 30b).

This man and his family join the growing host of Christians,
and the next day Paul and Silas are released and leave for Thessalonica. From there they travel to Berea, then on to Athens.

In Athens, the people give Paul the opportunity to speak at the
Areopagus, the prestigious center of Greek learning. What a thrill-
ing moment for Paul! But what a crushing defeat too. With his

whole heart, he tells them of the one true God; but many of them sneer at him (17:19–34). Only a few become Christians in Athens. It must have been discouraging for Paul.

Though his spirits are dampened, he pushes on to Corinth. Here he meets Aquila and Priscilla, tentmakers like himself, and they welcome him into their home and become strong believers. During his stay with them, he writes two letters to comfort the persecuted believers in Thessalonica and receives another vision from the Lord.

> And the Lord said to Paul . . . , "Do not be afraid any longer, but go on speaking and do not be silent; for I am with you, and no man will attack you in order to harm you, for I have many people in this city." (18:9–10)

With this reassurance, Paul stays on in Corinth for about a year and a half. Afterward, with Aquila and Priscilla at his side, he sails across the Aegean Sea to Ephesus. Here for only a short while, he then concludes his second journey by traveling back to Jerusalem and then to Antioch of Syria.

The Third Missionary Journey

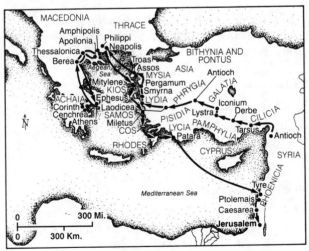

Paul's Third Missionary Journey[4]

4. *Life Application® Bible,* p. 1989. Maps © 1986, 1988 by Tyndale House Publishers, Inc. All rights reserved. Used by permission.

After a rest in Antioch, Paul launches out again along the same overland route as before. He strengthens the newly established churches along the way and finally arrives in Ephesus (18:22–19:1). He stays here about three years (20:31) and writes two letters to the church in Corinth—one which has been lost, and the other which is our 1 Corinthians.

At this time also, Paul determines to proclaim Christ in Rome.[5] Eventually, God provides him the opportunity when he is arrested and taken to Rome for trial. But for now, he leaves Ephesus and follows his previous route through Macedonia. He writes another letter to the Corinthian believers, then travels down to see them in person. From Corinth he pens a letter to the believers whom he longs to visit in Rome, and then he heads back to Ephesus. On his way to Ephesus, he once again calls on the churches in Macedonia. After a tearful farewell, he sails from Ephesus to Tyre and on to Caesarea. The disciples warn him not to go to Jerusalem, but with characteristic boldness, Paul responds:

> "What are you doing, weeping and breaking my heart? For I am ready not only to be bound, but even to die at Jerusalem for the name of the Lord Jesus." (21:13)

His third journey ends with him arriving in Jerusalem. Here his enemies arrest him, and he is placed in chains and shipped off to proclaim the gospel in the city God has placed on his heart: Rome.

Lessons from the Survey

In this lesson, we've painted a mural of Paul's missionary journeys. The following chart summarizes the highlights.

First Journey

Scripture	13:1–14:28
Missionaries	Barnabas, Saul, John Mark
Highlights	• Elymas blinded in Paphos
	• John Mark abandons the mission
	• Persecution from Jews
	• Paul stoned in Lystra

---

5. With Nero having begun his reign of cruelty, Paul longed to encourage the persecuted Roman Christians. Also, he saw Rome as a launching point for disseminating the message of Christ to the remotest parts of the world.

- Churches established in Asia Minor

Second Journey

Scripture	15:36–18:22
Missionaries	Paul, Silas, Timothy, Luke
Highlights	• Visit to churches in Asia Minor
	• Paul's vision of the man from Macedonia
	• Philippian jailer converts to Christianity
	• Paul preaches in Athens
	• Paul writes 1 and 2 Thessalonians in Corinth

Third Journey

Scripture	18:23–21:17
Missionaries	Paul, Luke, Timothy, and others (20:4)
Highlights	• Paul stays about three years in Ephesus
	• Paul writes 1 Corinthians
	• Riot in Ephesus
	• Paul writes 2 Corinthians from Macedonia and Romans from Corinth
	• Paul returns to Jerusalem

Later we'll move in closer to study the details; but for now, let the overall image impress you with three main principles.

First, achieving God's major objective means somebody has to be willing to go. Somebody has to be the Paul or Barnabas or Silas in order to accomplish God's mission for the world. It won't happen if all of us sit at home, enjoying the familiar. *Second,* when we walk in obedience, it doesn't mean we'll be preserved from trouble. Opposition often results from doing the will of God. *Third,* enduring a trial increases our vision. Trials cement our resolve to proclaim the gospel. They confirm the words of Paul in our own hearts:

> "I am ready not only to be bound, but even to die
> . . . for the name of the Lord Jesus." (Acts 21:13)

 Living Insights STUDY ONE

Paul could leave the security of the familiar and venture into the unknown because he had courageous faith. Read the following verses and write down the source of Paul's boldness.

2 Corinthians 4:13–15 _____

Ephesians 6:18–20 _____

1 Thessalonians 2:1–4 _____

2 Timothy 1:7–8 _____

Are you facing some unknowns? What are they?

_____

_____

From Paul's principles of courageous faith, what can you do to develop the boldness to enter your unknowns?

_____

_____

_____

🏵 *Living Insights*   STUDY TWO

What would silence your witness? Would a cynical look stop you? A laugh? A cold shoulder?

These kinds of responses from non-Christians can feel like stones pelting our spirits. It hurts when our neighbors overlook us for the block party, when we lose an account at work, or when a teacher mocks us because of our stand for Christ. We can become disillusioned and suddenly quiet about our faith.

Think back over our survey of Paul's journeys for a moment. Write down what the non-Christians did to silence his witness.

_____

_____

How did he respond to their abuses (see Acts 13:50–52)?

_____

_____

Nothing stopped Paul from proclaiming the gospel—not even

literal stoning (see 14:19–20). In what ways does his example inspire you to keep sharing your faith despite the hurts?

_____

_____

_____

_____

_____

_____

Chapter 9

WHEN THE GOING GETS ROUGH
Acts 13:4–13

When you became a Christian, did you think all the hard times would be over? Did you think the Christian life would be a kind of spiritual Disneyland, where worries are checked at the gate and the world is clean and pure and happy?

The truth is, life often gets rougher after we trust Christ. We feel new tensions between living in the kingdom of heaven and living in this world. We begin to see new truths—especially about ourselves—and this can make us uncomfortable. No, the frail bubble of idealism won't last long among reality's inevitable pinpricks. So, then, how can we be prepared to handle such difficulties?

The answer is not to swing to the other extreme and become a pessimist. Our creed shouldn't be Murphy's Law—"If anything can go wrong, it will" or "Smile. Tomorrow will be worse."[1] This approach to life may lower our expectations, but it also saps our joy.

Instead, it is better to be a realist, as F. B. Meyer counsels:

> Think it not strange, child of God, concerning the fiery trial that tries thee, as though some strange thing had happened. Rejoice! for it is a sure sign that thou art on the right track. If in an unknown country, I am informed that I must pass through a valley where the sun is hidden, or over a stony bit of road, to reach my abiding place—when I come to it, each moment of shadow or jolt of the carriage tells me that I am on the right road. So when a child of God passes through affliction he is not surprised.[2]

Saul was that kind of realist. John Mark, his young assistant, however, was more the dreamy idealist. Let's join these two missionaries and their companion Barnabas and find out what happened

---

1. Arthur Bloch, *The Complete Murphy's Law* (Los Angeles, Calif.: Price Stern Sloan, 1990), p. 5.

2. F. B. Meyer, *Christ in Isaiah* (Fort Washington, Pa.: Christian Literature Crusade, n.d.), p. 9.

when they encountered shadows and jolts on their first missionary journey.

A Good Beginning

No one had been on a missionary trip like this before. There were no books or diaries written by previous missionaries. There were no seminars on how to evangelize cross-culturally or what to say when the food tastes odd and the people behave differently. Like the pilgrims at Plymouth Rock, the three intrepid missionaries could only imagine what would await them. So they dreamed of people repenting and churches blossoming wherever they spoke about the Lord Jesus.

Filled with hope, they began their journey with great anticipation. The Holy Spirit had personally selected Barnabas and Saul, and they had decided to bring along John Mark as their companion. The assembly in Antioch supported the men, laying hands on them and sending them out with prayer and a host of good wishes.

They also had something even more important than the church's support: they had God's blessing (Acts 13:4a). What confidence and joy this must have brought them! Why, they could conquer the world for Christ! Theodore Epp gives us a glimpse of this kind of euphoria:

> Once a man is satisfied that he is in the center
> of God's plan and God is working out His will
> through him, that man is invincible.[3]

With God on their side, they couldn't lose. So they went to the port city of Seleucia, bought their tickets, and boarded the ship (v. 4b). Things were going great! Feeling unsinkable, they sailed smoothly to the island of Cyprus.

A Unique Island

Being a native, Barnabas knew Cyprus well. Cyprus means "copper," a name given the island because of the rich copper deposits. "It was sometimes called Makaria," noted William Barclay,

> which means the Happy Isle, because it was held
> that its climate was so perfect and its resources so

---

3. Theodore H. Epp, *Elijah, A Man of Like Nature* (Lincoln, Nebr.: A Back to the Bible Publication, 1965), p. 63.

varied that a man might find everything necessary for a happy life within its bounds.[4]

Cyprus was the Hawaii of the first century—not a bad place to visit on a missions trip! Certainly, its charisma must have impressed young John Mark when the men disembarked at Salamis, the largest city on the island. Once there, "they began to proclaim the word of God in the synagogues of the Jews" (v. 5b). But for all their trying, there is no record of any spiritual success in the large Jewish community.

Ministry in Cyprus, Pamphylia, and Galatia[5]

What could be wrong? Maybe they should try evangelizing the rural areas. So they went "through the whole island" (v. 6a).

Still no recorded converts.

A spiritual darkness in Cyprus was opposing their efforts. Through the centuries, the island had been ruled by the Egyptians, the Phoenicians, the Assyrians, the Persians, the Greeks, and the Romans. And under the hand of these nations, a pagan religious system developed. It centered around occultic magic and the licentious worship of a female deity—Aphrodite to the Greeks, Venus to the Romans. Consequently, Cyprus was a demon's playground.

A Difficult Experience

The by-now-disillusioned missionaries openly encountered these demonic powers when they arrived in Paphos, the capital city.

Opposition of Elymas

They found a certain magician, a Jewish false prophet whose name was Bar-Jesus, who was with

4. William Barclay, *The Acts of the Apostles*, rev. ed., The Daily Study Bible Series (Philadelphia, Pa.: Westminster Press, 1976), pp. 99–100.

5. *Life Application® Bible*, New International Version (copublishers; Wheaton, Ill.: Tyndale House Publishers, 1991 and Grand Rapids, Mich.: Zondervan Publishing House, 1991), p. 1978, 1980. Maps © 1986, 1988 by Tyndale House Publishers, Inc. All rights reserved. Used by permission.

the proconsul, Sergius Paulus, a man of intelligence. This man summoned Barnabas and Saul and sought to hear the word of God. But Elymas the magician (for thus his name is translated) was opposing them, seeking to turn the proconsul away from the faith. (vv. 6b–8)

Gaining an audience with the proconsul was a significant break-through for the gospel.[6] The Holy Spirit was working on this man's heart, but Satan was working too—through Bar-Jesus, who was also called Elymas.

Elymas means "the skillful one," and the root of Bar-Jesus means "son of salvation"—rather formidable titles. Sergius Paulus kept this powerful false prophet close by to forecast the future and decipher omens. Roman rulers, no matter how intelligent, were often super-stitious; and Elymas was profiting from this weakness, which is why he was so threatened by Saul's message. If Sergius Paulus converted to Christianity, it would spell the end of his own fame and power.

So Elymas stood against the missionaries, aggressively opposing them at every turn . . . trying his best to make his darkness over-come the light of Christ.

Confrontation by Paul

But Saul didn't back down. He was a realist. He faced this problem head-on.

Saul, who was also known as Paul,[7] filled with the Holy Spirit, fixed his gaze upon him, and said, "You who are full of all deceit and fraud, you son of the devil, you enemy of all righteousness, will you not cease to make crooked the straight ways of the Lord?" (vv. 9–10)

Like David on the battlefield with Goliath, Paul called Elymas an enemy of the Lord and let his stone fly.

"And now, behold, the hand of the Lord is upon you, and you will be blind and not see the sun for a

---

6. A proconsul was the governor of a Roman province.

7. Notice in verse 9 that the Apostle's name changes from Saul to Paul—from a Hebrew to a Gentile name. This change identified him as the Apostle to the Gentiles and signified his new role as the leader.

time." And immediately a mist and a darkness fell upon him, and he went about seeking those who would lead him by the hand. (v. 11)

Salvation of Paulus

God blinded the magician because he refused to see the truth. But the proconsul longed to see the truth, so God opened his eyes.

> The proconsul believed when he saw what had happened, being amazed at the teaching of the Lord. (v. 12)

The miracle impressed him, but the gospel amazed him. The miracle served to distinguish the false from the true prophet. But it was the gospel message that sparked new life in his spirit as he surrendered himself to Christ.

The proconsul's conversion filled the missionaries' drooping sails with encouragement as they left Sergius Paulus and the island of Cyprus for Pamphylia.

A Returned Missionary

Looking forward to smooth sailing from here on, they were surprised to encounter such severe problems that one of them packed up and returned home.

> Now Paul and his companions put out to sea from Paphos and came to Perga in Pamphylia; and John left them and returned to Jerusalem. (v. 13)

Luke records the incident with stark brevity. But from his words, we can piece together a theory concerning why John Mark suddenly left for Jerusalem.

First, notice Luke says "Paul and his companions." Until now, it had been "Barnabas and Saul" (see 12:25 and 13:2). Apparently, after his confrontation with Elymas, Paul had taken the lead. This shift might have perturbed John Mark, who was Barnabas' relative.[8]

Also, Pamphylia was a treacherous region. The coastal area around Perga was rife with disease, including malaria. It is possibly here that Paul suffered an ailment he later referred to in his epistle to the Galatians:

---

8. John Mark was Barnabas' cousin (Col. 4:10) and the son of Mary, who owned the house where the meeting was held to pray for Peter's freedom (Acts 12:12).

But you know that it was because of a bodily illness
that I preached the gospel to you the first time.
(4:13)

What bodily illness forced Paul inland, farther into Galatia? If he had contracted malaria in Perga, that would have been ample motivation to escape the lowlands to recover in the cooler mountain regions.[9] Perhaps that is why he decided they would head into the great Taurus mountain range, and the only way was a road notorious for danger from thieves.

All this undoubtedly added up to unbearable stress for John Mark. The lackluster response in Salamis and the demonic opposition in Paphos were enough to deflate him. But when sudden change, disease, and danger met him in Perga, any remaining courage fell to pieces. With his dreams shattered, idealistic John Mark could not handle the hard times.

Later, Paul would call John Mark's return to Jerusalem a desertion (Acts 15:38). It was a stormy, hurtful experience and a reminder of the importance of being prepared when the going gets rough.

Some Practical Conclusions

This story prepares us for those rough times in two ways. First, it teaches us that *there is no accomplishment without determination.* Whenever we are tempted to quit before the final bell—whether it's finishing school, completing a job, or riding out rough seas in family life—we won't achieve God's purpose without determining to persevere.

As a corollary, this story also reminds us that *there is no burden too heavy for Christ to carry.* No matter how determined you may be, the Taurus Mountains in your life may still overwhelm you. At these times, don't quit. Rather, by faith give your burden over to the One who faced His own mountain—Mount Calvary. He bore the cross; He can bear your fears as well.

---

9. Barclay identifies Paul's illness as malaria and associates it with his "thorn in the flesh" (2 Cor. 12:7–8). "The oldest tradition is that Paul suffered from prostrating headaches. And the most likely explanation is that he was the victim of a virulent recurring malaria fever which haunted the low coastal strip of Asia Minor. A traveller says that the headache characteristic of this malaria was like a red-hot bar thrust through the forehead." *The Acts of the Apostles,* pp. 101–2.

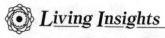

Can you imagine the intensity of John Mark's emotions? Fear, shame, and guilt must have crushed his spirit. Fortunately, though, his story does not end in failure. Barnabas takes him on another missionary trip to Cyprus (15:39). There he confronts his fears and grows strong. Later, even Paul recognizes his value to the cause of Christ, saying to Timothy, "Pick up Mark and bring him with you, for he is useful to me for service" (2 Tim. 4:11b). He makes a comeback.

Maybe you are battling failure right now. If so, there is hope. You can face your fears in God's strength, just like Mark did. And like him, you can make your own comeback.

Comeback

My fears have become a funnel cloud,
Whirling, whipping, choking me,
The debris of past pain
Spinning violently.

But I hear You calling:
"Come after Me."

How? I can't see You,
I can't touch You.
Give me Your hand at least.

"Hear My voice, and come."
So I step one small step.
The cloud roars around me,
Mocking my tiny faith
I step again.
It roars, but weaker this time.
Again and again I step,
The cloud slowly dwindling down.

When it is finally gone, the air is still and sweet.
I can breathe.
I can see.
And I can't believe how far I've come.
                                        —Bryce Klabunde

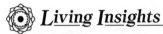

When the road became rough in Pamphylia, why were Paul and Barnabas able to keep going while John Mark broke down? Maybe it was because they were realistic about the hard times, while John Mark was too idealistic. Let's take a moment to contrast these two approaches to coping with difficult circumstances.

Idealists	Realists
• Believe everything will go smoothly.	• Recognize that problems are a normal, expected part of life.
• Are not prepared to handle problems, because they don't anticipate any.	• Can think on their feet, because they have already reckoned with the possibility of problems.
• Get taken by surprise and often feel overwhelmed.	• Start making plans to deal with the situation.
• Can be submarined, done in by the situation.	• Cope with the problems and overcome them.

How would you characterize your approach to life? Do you wear rose-colored glasses that tint everything beautiful and cut out all of life's glaring pains and frustrations? Or do you cultivate the insight to accept life as it comes?

_____

_____

If you struggle with the unavoidable disappointment and disillusionment broken ideals bring but still cling to your idealism, what do you think is making you hold on so tightly? Are you afraid of losing something? Are you equating realism with pessimism? What do you think it is?

_____

_____

_____

How can you become more of a realist?

_____

Remember, wanting to believe the best about people and situations, like John Mark did, is admirable. But that attitude needs to be tempered by the ability to accept the flaws and frustrations of reality—an approach to life that will keep you going on the sometimes rough roads you'll travel.

Chapter 10

A HUNGER FOR THE TRUTH

Acts 13:14–52

There's a famine in our land. You can't see it on our farms, where the wheat grows thick and the cornstalks reach toward heaven. You can't see it in our grocery stores either, where bottles and boxes and cans and cartons crowd the shelves. Neither can you see it on our dinner tables, where matching bowls and plates overflow with scrumptious delights. But still, there's a famine in the land.

The Old Testament prophet Amos tells us where we *can* see this famine.

> "Behold, days are coming," declares the Lord God,
> "When I will send a famine on the land,
> Not a famine for bread or a thirst for water,
> But rather for hearing the words of the Lord.
> And people will stagger from sea to sea,
> And from the north even to the east;
> They will go to and fro to seek the word of the
> Lord,
> But they will not find it." (Amos 8:11–12)

This is a famine for hearing the truth of God in words people can understand. It's not necessarily a dearth of preachers and programs and Bibles and churches; but a hunger for clear, accurate, practical teaching of the living words of God.

As in our day, Paul's day also showed the signs of spiritual famine. In this lesson, we'll see him model how to share the bread of Christ with needy people—people like our friends and family, who, now more than ever, hunger for the truth.

Orientation: Geography and History

From our previous lesson, you may recall how hungrily Sergius Paulus had taken in the truth. So Paul, wanting to feed more people in the same way, directed his companions toward Perga. Young John Mark, however, abruptly abandoned the mission there. Disappointed but determined, the elder missionaries turned toward Pisidian Antioch, a prestigious and strategically located Roman colony in southern Galatia. "In bringing the gospel to Pisidian Antioch," Merrill Unger observed,

> Paul and Barnabas were planting the witness in a communication nerve center in the heart of Asia Minor through which an [east-west] traffic artery ran. Westward it connected with . . . the Greek world of the Aegean. Eastward it gave access to Lystra, Derbe and via the Cilician Gates led on to Tarsus, Issus and Antioch-on-the-Orontes.[1]

The missionaries' strategy was to preach the gospel here, allowing it to flow through Asia Minor and be carried along by new believers. But how would they start? There was no welcoming committee to greet them when they arrived. There was no advance team putting up posters and planning guest spots and lectures for them. They had only one point of contact: the local synagogue. So, "on the Sabbath day they went into the synagogue and sat down" (Acts 13:14b).

What a gracious way to begin. They didn't burst onto the scene with their gospel-guns blazing. They politely waited for God to give them an opportunity.

Proclamation: Survey and Offer

Sure enough, the chance for presenting their message came.

> After the reading of the Law and the Prophets the synagogue officials sent to them, saying, "Brethren, if you have any word of exhortation for the people, say it." (v. 15)

Do they have any word of exhortation? What a question! Praising the Lord for this delicious opportunity,

> Paul stood up, and motioning with his hand, he said,
>   "Men of Israel, and you who fear God, listen."
> (v. 16)

He doesn't say, "Listen up, you reprobates. I've got what you need, so you better pay attention!" No, he speaks kindly and with respect.

---

1. Merrill F. Unger, *Unger's Bible Handbook* (Chicago, Ill.: Moody Press, 1966), p. 580.

What follows shows his mastery of communicating the gospel. He will begin where his listeners are—on their parched, barren island where they are starving for truth. Then he will fashion his ideas into a bridge, taking them to the plush, green island of Christ. There he will show them the luscious fruit of the gospel. But he doesn't stop, for one more destination awaits: the island of response. If they respond in faith, the sumptuous freedom and forgiveness found in Christ will be theirs to enjoy.

With this three-island outline in mind, let's examine Paul's sermon up close.

Abraham to Jesus

The foundation of Paul's bridge to Christ is set deep in Scripture. In alluding to and quoting from several Old Testament books, Paul lends authority to his words and also builds on the bedrock of the familiar with his audience. Let's trace what he says.

Paul's Words	Their Source
"The God of this people Israel chose our fathers,	Genesis
and made the people great during their stay in the land of Egypt, and with an uplifted arm He led them out from it.	Exodus
And for a period of about forty years He put up with them in the wilderness.	Leviticus, Numbers, Deuteronomy
And when He had destroyed seven nations in the land of Canaan, He distributed their land as an inheritance—all of which took about four hundred and fifty years.	Joshua
And after these things He gave them judges	Judges
until Samuel the prophet. And then they asked for a king, and God gave them Saul the son of Kish, a man of the tribe of Benjamin, for forty years. And after He had removed him, He raised up David to be their king, concerning whom He also testified and said, 'I have found David the son of Jesse, a man after My heart, who will do all My will.'" (Acts 13:17–22)	1 Samuel, 2 Samuel

The people nod in agreement. He has them interested—he's playing a tune they all know and love. But then he adds a new strain they've never heard before.

"From the offspring of this man, according to promise, God has brought to Israel a Savior, Jesus." (v. 23)

A Savior? Who is this Jesus? The people lean forward, their ears
burning to hear more.

Crucifixion and Resurrection

Sensing their interest, Paul develops this new theme by telling
them about Jesus' forerunner, John the Baptist (vv. 24–25). Then
he pauses. He has brought them to the island of Christ, and like a
tour guide, he announces what they are about to see.

"Brethren, sons of Abraham's family, and those
among you who fear God, to us the word of this
salvation is sent out." (v. 26)

Acknowledging his kinship with the people by addressing them
as brethren, Paul broaches the subject to which he has led them—
the spiritual food to satisfy their famished souls. Next, instead of
dumping the truth on them he lays it out before them like a banquet,
carefully presenting each aspect of the salvation story. He has already set the table; so now, on a silver tray, he offers them the
delicacies of the gospel: the crucifixion (vv. 27–29), the resurrection
(vv. 30–34), David's prophecy—"Thou wilt not allow Thy Holy
One to undergo decay"— and how it is fulfilled in Christ (vv. 35, 37).

His audience sits in wonder. But Paul does not let them rest: a
final island awaits.

Forgiveness and Freedom

"Therefore let it be known to you, brethren, that
through Him forgiveness of sins is proclaimed to you,
and through Him everyone who believes is freed
from all things, from which you could not be freed
through the Law of Moses." (vv. 38–39)

On this island, Paul shows them that the Law chains them to
failure and sin. Then he points out that Christ's forgiveness frees
them to worship God and enjoy His benefits. Now they must choose
between the two.

Reaction: Acceptance and Rejection

The people are amazed at what they have heard. But how will

they respond to Paul's message?

Invitation to Return

No altar call or closing hymn follows Paul's sermon; he and Barnabas gather their things and start to leave. The people, however,

> kept begging that these things might be spoken to them the next Sabbath. Now when the meeting of the synagogue had broken up, many of the Jews and of the God-fearing proselytes followed Paul and Barnabas, who, speaking to them, were urging them to continue in the grace of God. (vv. 42–43)

Paul's words had opened the kitchen door, and the aroma of spiritual food on the stove had awakened the ferocious hunger in the people.

> And the next Sabbath nearly the whole city assembled to hear the word of God. (v. 44)

However, not everyone was as enthusiastic.

Opposition from Jews

> When the Jews saw the crowds, they were filled with jealousy, and began contradicting the things spoken by Paul, and were blaspheming. (v. 45)

Did the missionaries panic? Not at all; a famine was in the land, and there were plenty of other people who craved the gospel. So instead of trying to convert those who weren't interested, they turned their attention and action to those who were. A good lesson for us to learn as well.

> And Paul and Barnabas spoke out boldly and said, "It was necessary that the word of God should be spoken to you first; since you repudiate it, and judge yourselves unworthy of eternal life, behold, we are turning to the Gentiles. For thus the Lord has commanded us,
> 'I have placed You as a light for the Gentiles,
> That You should bring salvation to the end of the earth.'"
> And when the Gentiles heard this, they began rejoicing and glorifying the word of the Lord; and as

many as had been appointed to eternal life believed. And the word of the Lord was being spread through the whole region.[2] But the Jews aroused the devout women of prominence and the leading men of the city, and instigated a persecution against Paul and Barnabas, and drove them out of their district. But they shook off the dust of their feet in protest against them and went to Iconium. (vv. 46–51)

Rejoicing of Disciples

As Paul and Barnabas left for the next spot on the map, they heard shouts of jealousy echoing behind them, but they also heard shouts of joy. For

the disciples were continually filled with joy and with the Holy Spirit. (v. 52)

We can't have true joy without the Holy Spirit. He's the One who causes us to hunger, then fills us with Christ, the Savior of the world.

Application: Hungry and Full

Are you hungry for the freedom and forgiveness Christ has to offer? By faith, accept the truth of His sin-atoning death and life-giving resurrection.

"Through Him forgiveness of sins is proclaimed to you, and through Him everyone who believes is freed from all things." (vv. 38b–39a)

Maybe you are already spiritually full. If you have received Christ's forgiveness, pass the Bread of Life along and show others where to find it. In these days of famine, people desperately need what you have to offer.

---

2. The Greek tense of the verb translated "was being spread" suggests that the gospel was continually being spread as people traveled in and out of Antioch.

"Happiness," Graham Greene wrote,

> is like one of those islands far out in the Pacific which has been reported by sailors when it emerges from the haze where no cartographer has ever marked it. The island disappears again for a generation, but no navigator can be quite certain that it only existed in the imagination of some long-dead lookout.[3]

Perhaps lately you have been searching for happiness in relationships, things, prestige, or pleasure. But these bearings have led you nowhere; happiness is still out there in the haze.

The new believers in this lesson found true happiness in the forgiveness and freedom described by Paul (see Acts 13:38–39). Let's examine these two concepts more closely.

Read Colossians 2:13–14, where Paul expands the concept of forgiveness. From these verses, describe the forgiveness process.

_____

_____

In what ways can experiencing Christ's forgiveness produce lasting joy in your life?

_____

_____

_____

The other gift Christ offers is freedom (Acts 13:39). Literally, the word *freedom* here means "justification." As the NIV translates the verse,

> "Through him everyone who believes is justified from everything you could not be justified from by the law of Moses."

---

3. Graham Greene, *Doctor Fischer of Geneva or the Bomb Party* (New York, N.Y.: Simon and Schuster, 1980), p. 53.

The Law cannot justify. Only Christ can declare you free from the penalty of sin and free to live according to His example. Read Romans 8:1–4, where Paul discusses our freedom in depth. What does Christ free us from? How did He secure our freedom?

_____

_____

How do you think experiencing Christ's freedom produces lasting joy in your life?

_____

_____

_____

If you feel lost in the haze, follow God's Word to Christ. He is the only One who can offer you true joy.

◉ Living Insights STUDY TWO

None of us would hoard food while a friend starves. Yet we often keep the truth to ourselves even though our friend needs it desperately. Why do you think Christians are sometimes timid about sharing the gospel with their non-Christian friends or relatives?

_____

_____

_____

In today's passage, Paul modeled how to speak boldly about Christ. First, he tailored his message to the needs of his audience. He identified with them and grabbed their interest. What are the needs of those you know who aren't believers? Have you identified with them, cared about them—and communicated this? How do you think you can grab their interest?

_____

_____

_____

Second, Paul did not back up a truck and haphazardly dump the truth on them. He took time to prepare the food for them and lay out a banquet. Write down how you would logically present the gospel to an unbeliever, pointing them to Christ. We'll help you with an outline.

All have sinned: _____

_____

Penalty for sin: _____

_____

Provision of Christ: _____

_____

Requirement of faith: _____

_____

Third, Paul spoke kindly. He was confident in his message, but he never forced it on his hearers. Consequently, the people wanted to hear more. How can you show respect when talking to non-Christians?

_____

_____

Like the Jews who became jealous of Paul, not everyone will receive the truth you share. So focus your energies on those who seem most open, and pray for those who raise angry defenses. One day they, too, may realize just how hungry they really are.

Chapter 11

OPERATION YO-YO

Acts 14:1–20

T hrough It All," a moving song written from the heart of Andraé
Crouch, capsulizes the message of Paul's life.

> I've had many tears and sorrows,
> I've had questions for tomorrow,
> There've been times I didn't know right from
> wrong.
> But in ev'ry situation,
> God gave blessed consolation
> that my trials come to only make me strong.

> I've been to lots of places
> And I've seen a lot of faces,
> There've been times I felt so all alone.
> But in my lonely hours,
> Yes, those precious lonely hours
> Jesus let me know that I was His own.

> I thank God for the mountains
> And I thank Him for the valleys,
> I thank Him for the storms He brought me
> through.
> For if I'd never had a problem,
> I wouldn't know that He could solve them,
> I'd never know what faith in God could do.

> Through it all,
> Through it all,
> Oh, I've learned to trust in Jesus,
> I've learned to trust in God.
> Through it all,
> Through it all,
> I've learned to depend upon His Word.[1]

---

1. Andraé Crouch, "Through It All," © Copyright 1971 by MANNA MUSIC, INC., 25510
Ave. Stanford, Valencia, Calif., 91355. International copyright secured. All rights reserved.
Used by permission.

Not around it, not over it—but *through* success and failure, *through* joy and sorrow, Paul learned to trust God and depend upon His Word. In Paul's own words,

> I have learned to be content in whatever circum-stances I am. I know how to get along with humble means, and I also know how to live in prosperity; in any and every circumstance I have learned the secret of being filled and going hungry, both of having abundance and suffering need. I can do all things through Him who strengthens me. (Phil. 4:11b–13)

In the following passage Paul models what he learned, demon-strating the stability needed during life's ups and downs. He shows us how we, too, can follow Christ . . . through it all.

The Memory of Pisidian Antioch

Paul and Barnabas had just come off of a very mixed experience in Pisidian Antioch. Many of the people there had enthusiastically accepted Paul's message of salvation through Christ, but some of the Jews had instigated a persecution against Paul and Barnabas, and driven them out of their district (see Acts 13:50b).

In spite of the rough treatment, the two missionaries and their new Christian friends "were continually filled with joy and with the Holy Spirit" (v. 52b). The opposition hadn't dampened their spirits; rather, they left town riding the winds of success.

The Evangelism of New Fields

Their next mission-ary field, Iconium, was equally fertile. Even the land teemed with life— sheep grazed quietly, flax fields rippled in the breeze . . . all signs of fruitful times ahead.

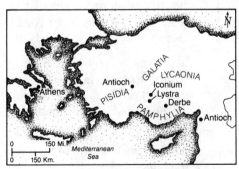

Continued Ministry in Galatia[2]

2. *Life Application® Bible*, New International Version (copublishers; Wheaton, Ill: Tyndale House Publishers, 1991 and Grand Rapids, Mich.: Zondervan Publishing House, 1991), p. 1982. Maps © 1986, 1988 by Tyndale House Publishers, Inc. All rights reserved. Used by permission.

Iconium

Paul and Barnabas began their ministry in Iconium where all experienced evangelists do: where there are many people.

> They entered the synagogue of the Jews together, and spoke in such a manner that a great multitude believed, both of Jews and of Greeks. (14:1b)

Referring to the Gentiles as "Greeks," Luke hints at the strong Hellenistic flavor present in this ancient city.

> Iconium, in spite of becoming a Roman colony under Hadrian, remained predominately Greek in tone and somewhat resistant toward Roman influence. . . . With the organizing of the province of Galatia, Iconium became an independent unit. . . . As a Greek city, Iconium was governed by its assembly of citizens.[3]

These citizens embraced the gospel at first. But following a chain of events that would become a typical pattern in Paul's ministry,

> the Jews who disbelieved stirred up the minds of the Gentiles, and embittered them against the brethren. (v. 2)

This situation was especially dangerous because of Iconium's citizen-run government. The assembly had the power to condemn and execute the missionaries without Rome's involvement. So Paul and Barnabas had once again yo-yoed from high to low, delight to disaster. But they did not despair. Rather,

> they spent a long time there speaking boldly *with reliance upon the Lord*, who was bearing witness to the word of His grace, granting that signs and wonders be done by their hands. (v. 3, emphasis added)

Their response demonstrated the key to remaining stable: *they relied upon the Lord.* If they didn't rely on the Lord in times of elation, they would fly pridefully high; in times of discouragement,

3. E. M. Blaiklock, "Iconium," *The Zondervan Pictorial Encyclopedia of the Bible*, ed. Merrill C. Tenney (Grand Rapids, Mich.: Zondervan Publishing House, Regency Reference Library, 1976), vol. 3, pp. 240–41.

they would hurtle perilously low. But by depending on Jesus, they would be able to pull through it all.

How can we, like Paul and Barnabas, rely upon the Lord? By learning to focus on His Word. The Lord and His Word—not people and circumstances—build a stable foundation to help us withstand the winds of change that sometimes threaten to blow us over.

While remaining fixed on the Lord, Paul and Barnabas had to make a quick decision because the sentiment simmering against them in Iconium had reached a boiling point.

> The multitude of the city was divided; and some sided with the Jews, and some with the apostles. And when an attempt was made by both the Gentiles and the Jews with their rulers, to mistreat and to stone them, they became aware of it and fled to the cities of Lycaonia, Lystra and Derbe, and the surrounding region. (vv. 4–6)

Could these be the same people who had earlier welcomed them so eagerly? Now they wanted to stone them! Rather than face the heat, Paul and Barnabas wisely left the city.[4]

Lystra

The winds of circumstance had been in their favor when they came to Iconium, but a storm of hatred drove them to the next city, Lystra. In spite of the extremes, however, "they continued to preach the gospel" (v. 7). What stability! In the turbulence, they tied themselves to the helm and stayed on the course God had given them.

Lystra, however, was different than Iconium. Among other things, there were not enough Jews to establish a synagogue, so the missionaries ministered on the streets to the unreached pagans. Consequently, unexpected and jarring events occurred that sent Paul and Barnabas soaring up and then crashing down again. Precipitating this new roller coaster ride was a miracle performed by Paul.

At Lystra there was sitting a certain man, without

---

4. Did the missionaries lack faith because they escaped when their lives were threatened? No, their actions demonstrated the use of common sense in determining God's will. Since God had provided them a way of escape, to stay would have been foolish.

strength in his feet, lame from his mother's womb, who had never walked. This man was listening to Paul as he spoke, who, when he had fixed his gaze upon him, and had seen that he had faith to be made well, said with a loud voice, "Stand upright on your feet." And he leaped up and began to walk. And when the multitudes saw what Paul had done, they raised their voice, saying in the Lycaonian language, "The gods have become like men and have come down to us." And they began calling Barnabas, Zeus, and Paul, Hermes, because he was the chief speaker. And the priest of Zeus, whose temple was just outside the city, brought oxen and garlands to the gates, and wanted to offer sacrifice with the crowds. (vv. 8–13)

Unknowingly, Paul had awakened a sleeping giant from the legends of these pagan people, which caused them to assume that he and Barnabas were gods. William Barclay explains.

The people round Lystra told a story that once Zeus and Hermes had come to this earth in disguise. None in all the land would give them hospitality until at last two old peasants, Philemon and his wife Baucis, took them in. As a result the whole population was wiped out by the gods except Philemon and Baucis, who were made the guardians of a splendid temple and were turned into two great trees when they died. So when Paul healed the crippled man the people of Lystra were determined not to make the same mistake again.[5]

The Iconians had just kicked them out of town in disgrace, but now these Lycaonians were treating them like gods. How vulnerable to pride Paul and Barnabas must have been when this flattery suddenly launched them from the status of outlaws to that of royalty. Yet the missionaries kept their perspective.

When the apostles, Barnabas and Paul, heard of it, they tore their robes and rushed out into the crowd,

5. William Barclay, *The Acts of the Apostles*, rev. ed., The Daily Study Bible Series (Philadelphia, Pa.: Westminster Press, 1976), p. 109.

crying out and saying, "Men, why are you doing these things? We are also men of the same nature as you." (vv. 14–15a)

The missionaries wanted off the pedestal on which the people were placing them—a struggle that many in today's ministry face, as Lloyd John Ogilvie notes.

> We put the communicator on a pedestal and evade the communication. We have a seemingly limitless capacity to give the honor that belongs to Christ to the people who seek to introduce us to him. Pastors, parents, friends, and teachers who have brought us the good news are often made the source of our security. We elevate them to supersainthood and miss for ourselves the dynamic that has made them admirable. We make matinee idols out of Christian leaders and forget that the greatest honor we can pay them is to become what we admire in them. . . . The reason there are so many prima donnas in the pulpit is that we have given the messenger more honor than the message.[6]

Trying to draw their attention away from himself and into his message, Paul announced to the crowd:

> "[We] preach the gospel to you in order that you should turn from these vain things to a living God, who made the heaven and the earth and the sea, and all that is in them. And in the generations gone by He permitted all the nations to go their own ways; and yet He did not leave Himself without witness, in that He did good and gave you rains from heaven and fruitful seasons, satisfying your hearts with food and gladness." (vv. 15b–17)

In his address, Paul explained that there is one true God who has given people freedom of choice. But, although humanity has chosen sin, God in His grace has not allowed sin's consequences to get out of hand. He blesses all people in spite of their sin. Did this bring the Lystrans to reason? Luke tells us that

6. Lloyd John Ogilvie, *Drumbeat of Love* (Waco, Tex.: Word Books, Publisher, 1976), p. 187.

even saying these things, they with difficulty re-strained the crowds from offering sacrifice to them. (v. 18)

Then, in the midst of the uproar, "Jews came from Antioch and Iconium, and . . . won over the multitudes" (v. 19a). Suddenly, the fawning adulation turned into hateful jeers. Like wild animals that eat out of your hand one moment and bite you the next, the people bared their teeth at the missionaries and "stoned Paul and dragged him out of the city, supposing him to be dead" (v. 19b).

The garlands had become jagged stones, bruising and gashing Paul's body. A moment ago he was a god; now he was a dog to be cornered, killed, and tossed onto a dung heap outside the city. Paul later recalled for the Corinthian believers the horror of the situation:

> I think you ought to know, dear brothers, about the hard time we went through in Asia. We were really crushed and overwhelmed, and feared we would never live through it. We felt we were doomed to die. (2 Cor. 1:8–9a TLB)

This was Paul's lowest valley. He was enduring the same kind of brutality that killed Stephen, the martyr whom he had once eagerly watched die in Jerusalem. However, this stoning would not write the final chapter of his life.

> While the disciples stood around him, he arose and entered the city. And the next day he went away with Barnabas to Derbe. (Acts 14:20)

Opening his eyes, Paul saw the concerned faces of a small group of Christians. The Apostle's testimony had borne fruit in the lives of a few townspeople, among whom were young Timothy, his mother, and grandmother (see 2 Tim. 1:5). They had come here to the trash heap, expecting to find Paul bloodied and dead. Amazed that he was still alive, they saw him rise slowly to his feet.[7] Then, despite the pain, he went right back into the city and, the next morning, on to Derbe.

---

7. Did God resurrect Paul from the dead? Probably not, because Luke says the people *supposed* he was dead (v. 19b), and he does not counter that opinion in the next verse. Certainly, though, God preserved Paul in an amazing—if not miraculous—way.

The Value of Personal Stability

Stable, determined, unswerving—these words describe Paul and Barnabas. Neither the peaks of success and popularity nor the swamps of failure and ignominy could alter their resolve to proclaim Christ. Their examples provide several lessons for us as we face the strains and pains of our own ups and downs.

First, we learn that *failure and discouragement call for perspective and vision.* There will be an end to hard times, and we must keep the perspective that our whole life isn't ruined by one failure or rejection.

Second, *success and elation must be tempered with reality and humility.* We must remember, as Spurgeon wrote, "that it is God who accomplishes the work, that He can continue to do so without my help, and that He will be able to make out with other means whenever He cuts me down to size." [8]

Third, Paul and Barnabas remind us that *balance requires stability.* When the winds of change gust and swirl around us, we need firm footing to keep our balance. Such steadiness comes through the stability of relying on the Lord, *through it all.* This kind of trust is summed up in Paul's words to the Corinthians,

> We felt we were doomed to die and saw how powerless we were to help ourselves; but that was good, for then we put everything into the hands of God, who alone could save us, for he can even raise the dead. And he did help us, and saved us from a terrible death; yes, and we expect him to do it again and again. (2 Cor. 1:9–10 TLB)

 Living Insights

How quickly the ups and downs of life can come upon us!

How head-spinningly swift, "Hail, Zeus! Hail, Hermes! Receive our homage, O magnificent gods, and accept the humble sacrifice of your worthless servants!" can turn to, "Stone him! Stone him!"

How shocking for this to happen to the servants of the Most High God! Or is it? Life's yo-yo reeled and pitched the very Son of

---

8. Charles Haddon Spurgeon, as quoted by J. Oswald Sanders in *Spiritual Leadership*, rev. ed. (Chicago, Ill.: Moody Press, 1980), p. 231.

the Most High God as well. Meditate for a few moments on His experiences in Matthew 21:6–9 and 27:20, 22–23.

Have you ever gone from being on top of the world one moment to being at the bottom of the heap the next? Try to put one such experience into words, remembering your thoughts, feelings, and actions.

_____

_____

_____

How firm was your footing? Did either of these extremes topple your balance? Your faith?

_____

_____

Extremes will always be a part of life, but we needn't be at their mercy. Keeping the right perspective can be a key in maintaining our stability. Compare Paul's words in Acts 14:15–17 with a few glimpses from Jesus' life in Matthew 21:12–13; 26:39, 42, 44; and Luke 23:34a, 46. What is the common focus present in their experiences?

_____

_____

How can Paul's and Christ's focus become more your own?

_____

_____

_____

⊛ *Living Insights*   STUDY TWO

In Galatians, Paul's letter to his first converts, Paul alludes to the stoning he received in Lystra: "I bear on my body the brand-marks of Jesus" (6:17b). His scars were badges of his commitment to Christ.

94

You may have your own set of scars. Perhaps you gave Christ's love to someone in need, but that person gave you heartache in return. Maybe you stood against slander aimed at your friend, only to receive ridicule yourself. What scars do you bear for Christ? List them here.

_____

_____

_____

After Paul's stoning, he could have hobbled onto the fastest boat for home and no one would have blamed him. But Christ gave him the courage to go on. Do you feel like giving up? How can you go on in spite of your past pain?

_____

_____

_____

Chapter 12

WRAPPING UP A
MEMORABLE TRIP
Acts 14:21–28

"M y son is home!" In her apron and woolen sweater, the mother leans over the porch railing, her arms outstretched, welcoming her son home from the war. She is the central figure in Norman Rockwell's painting *Homecoming GI.* The young soldier she longs to hug stands in the foreground in his outgrown uniform, facing his ramshackle tenement home. His little brother darts down the stairs to see him, and his sisters squeal with excitement. The neighbors, too, peer out windows, over fences, and around corners. Off to the side, his sweetheart stands against the wall, smiling shyly—"He's home."

This *Saturday Evening Post* cover captured the homecoming dreams of families all over America at the close of World War II. Centuries before, battle-weary Paul and Barnabas had also dreamed of their homecoming day. Soon, the Holy Spirit having punched their return tickets, they would be standing before family and friends, feeling the warmth of home.

A Quick Review

The two missionaries had been away for months. They had journeyed from Antioch of Syria to Cyprus, preached Christ throughout the island, confronted Elymas the Sorcerer, and converted the governor. Then they had sailed to Perga, where Paul became ill—probably with malaria—and John Mark abandoned the mission. Then up the Taurus Mountains they had gone to Pisidian Antioch, the crossroads of inland Asia Minor. Iconium was their next stop, then pagan Lystra—where they were worshiped as gods before Paul was stoned and left for dead.

Miraculously surviving the stoning, Paul went on with Barnabas to Derbe. There they "preached the gospel" and "made many disciples" (Acts 14:21a), and there they also sensed God's timing to return to Antioch of Syria. Now, we'll follow along as they backtrack through the cities they have just evangelized, visiting the newly established churches along the way.

A Profitable Return

This part of their missionary journey is easy to overlook, but it was a crucial aspect of the spread of Christianity. While the first part of their journey had been for evangelism, this last part is for edifying the young converts. These new believers had no seminars on the Christian life to attend, no church growth manuals to follow, no books or tapes—there wasn't even a New Testament to read!

So Paul and Barnabas gather their courage and retrace their trail of blood and heartache through Lystra, Iconium, and Pisidian Antioch to give the new churches vital spiritual instruction. As they travel and teach, they have a five-step plan for building up the believers—a plan we can follow in our homes and churches today.

They Strengthened Their Souls

Their first objective is to strengthen the new Christians.

> They returned to Lystra and to Iconium and to Antioch, strengthening the souls of the disciples. (vv. 21b–22a)

This word *strengthening*, rarely used in the New Testament, has been defined as "to make more firm, to give additional . . . strength."[1] We might say "to beef up"—to add strength to what is already present. These new believers have only had appetizers of truth for their nourishment; they now need a full-course meal to put meat on their spiritual bones.

So Paul and Barnabas devote themselves to teaching them. As they touch their lives, they shape them into godly men and women. These young Christians will need such strength to endure the inevitable trials awaiting them. They will also need encouragement—the missionaries' second objective.

They Encouraged Them to Persevere Realistically

As Paul and Barnabas return to each city, they spend time

> encouraging [the disciples] to continue in the faith, and saying, "Through many tribulations we must enter the kingdom of God." (v. 22b)

---

1. Archibald Thomas Robertson, *Word Pictures in the New Testament* (Grand Rapids, Mich.: Baker Book House, 1930), vol. 3, p. 216.

Notice that they don't paint a rosy, trouble-free future; they are preparing the believers for battle. These raw recruits need to understand the harsh reality of persecution. They need to know that tribulations will come, but that with the Lord they can persevere. "Hang in there," Paul and Barnabas are saying. "You can make it. Don't give up when the going gets tough." [2]

They Gave Assistance in the Realm of Organization

Few things are more frustrating than the lack of a clear plan and the leadership to carry it out. So, wisely, the missionaries "appointed elders for them in every church, having prayed with fasting" (v. 23a). Elders, or in Greek, *presbuteros*, were sometimes known as bishops or overseers—the office was the same (compare 20:17, 28). They had to be spiritually qualified according to the guidelines Paul later listed in 1 Timothy 3:1–7 and Titus 1:5–9.

Luke says that Paul and Barnabas "appointed" these elders. Explaining the meaning of the Greek word for *appoint*, A. T. Robertson wrote,

> Cheirotoneō (from *cheirotonos*, extending the hand, *cheir*, hand, and *teinō*, to stretch) is an old verb that originally meant to vote by show of the hands, finally to appoint with the approval of an assembly that chooses as in II Cor. 8:19, and then to appoint without regard to choice. [3]

So were the elders selected by congregational vote or literally appointed by Paul and Barnabas? We cannot be sure. But we do know that elders served a vital leadership role in the early church, as they do in churches today.

Sometimes, though, we quibble about these kinds of issues— how to select leaders, or how many leaders we should have, or what title we should give them. But unlike doctrine, these matters are flexible. Therefore we must be open to different styles of organization—as long as those styles advance, not hinder, the gospel of Christ.

---

2. Jesus had similarly encouraged His disciples: "In the world you have tribulation, but take courage; I have overcome the world" (John 16:33b).

3. Robertson, *Word Pictures in the New Testament*, p. 216.

They Entrusted Them to the Lord

We've seen Paul and Barnabas teach, encourage, and organize these young believers. Next they entrust them to God's care: "They commended them to the Lord in whom they had believed" (Acts 14:23b).

The Greek word for *commend* means "to deposit as in a bank."[4] The apostles entrusted their priceless newborn believers into the Lord's hands for safekeeping. This action highlighted God's trustworthiness as well as the danger of hero worship. Paul and Barnabas were just men; the people must place their faith in the Lord, not in them.

Only one more objective remained for Paul and Barnabas on their return trip. With their evangelism and edification work now completed, they simply had to finish the course.

They Finished What They Set Out to Accomplish

> And they passed through Pisidia and came into Pamphylia. And when they had spoken the word in Perga, they went down to Attalia; and from there they sailed to Antioch, from which they had been commended to the grace of God for the work that they had accomplished. (vv. 24–26)

For many months, Paul and Barnabas had been on their own. No one had followed them with clipboard in hand to keep them on schedule. They didn't send out any progress reports or monthly newsletters. Yet, the two travelers had been faithful to their

The End of the First Journey[5]

4. Robertson, *Word Pictures in the New Testament*, p. 218.

5. *Life Application® Bible*, New International Version (copublishers; Wheaton, Ill.: Tyndale House Publishers, 1991 and Grand Rapids, Mich.: Zondervan Publishing House, 1991), p. 1984. Maps © 1986, 1988 by Tyndale House Publishers, Inc. All rights reserved. Used by permission.

task. The Holy Spirit had commissioned them for a job, and they had done it—not by their own strength, but by "the grace of God."

An Exciting Report

Landing at Seleucia, they hike the last few miles to Antioch, their steps quickening the closer they come. How they long to bask in the fellowship of friends and family, to taste familiar food, to walk familiar streets . . . to be home.

> And when they had arrived and gathered the church together, they began to report all things that God had done with them and how He had opened a door of faith to the Gentiles. (v. 27)

Notice a subtle point Luke makes: "they . . . gathered the church together." He didn't say that they gathered the Christians into the church, but they gathered *the church.* To the early Christians, the church meant the people, not the building.

We say, "Let's go to church," but we *are* the church, and everywhere *we* go the church goes too. What we call "the church" is nothing more than a meeting place; God's true temple is made of flesh and bone, not brick and concrete (see 1 Cor. 6:19; Eph. 2:19–22).

As the church gathers together, Paul and Barnabas give a two-point report. First, *they emphasize what God has done.* They don't say, "We did this, then we did that." God was the one convicting hearts, nurturing faith, and implanting joy.

Second, *they announce how the Gentiles have believed.* God had opened wide the doors of faith so that now even pagans could enter the kingdom. This was amazing news in those days, for the Jews had faithfully guarded those doors for centuries. How rare it was for Gentiles to believe in the Jewish God—as rare as it is for Muslims or Hindus to trust Christ today. Think how incredible it would be if thousands of Muslims became Christians during a Billy Graham crusade in Baghdad. That was the impact the missionaries' report had on the people.

So together the church rejoices because of the gospel's life-changing power and God's protection of Paul and Barnabas. What a wonderful homecoming for these two men. Then the weary travelers settle in for a needed rest, spending "a long time with the disciples" (v. 28).

Application

In the last two chapters of Acts, we've strapped on our backpacks and hiked along with these missionaries across the island of Cyprus, all over Asia Minor, and back again. It's been a rewarding first missionary journey, and also a painful one. As we reflect on our trip, two lessons etch themselves on our tattered maps.

First, *it is at the end of a difficult experience that God reveals the benefits*. Another Apostle emphasized this point in his epistle to the believers in Asia Minor:

> And after you have suffered for a little while, the
> God of all grace, who called you to His eternal glory
> in Christ, will Himself perfect, confirm, strengthen
> and establish you. (1 Pet. 5:10)

In Paul's report, he must have marveled at what God had done through his sickness, John Mark's departure, the opposition, the stoning. The same is true for us when our storm passes and we can see clearly again. For after the suffering we realize that God has been perfecting, confirming, strengthening, and establishing us all along.

Second, *sometimes the ravages of sin preempt the blessing of God*. Paul's body may have borne the aches of sickness and the scars of stoning, but it was his heart that hurt the most. God had brought many to salvation, yet how many millions were still gripped in sin's clutches?

As Paul looked toward the west, the faces of these men and women in need of salvation flashed through his mind. One day he would go back to them and travel even further into Macedonia and Greece and eventually Rome itself. But for now, he could only dream, as we do, of an entire world knowing Christ.

 Living Insights

It must perturb God when a new believer withers for lack of care. The seed is planted, a tender shoot has sprouted, yet no one waters it or tills the soil. And eventually, it stops growing altogether. The tree it could become remains hidden within its pale stock and drooping leaves.

That's why Paul gave these instructions:

Older men are to be temperate, dignified, sensible, sound in faith, in love, in perseverance. Older women likewise are to be reverent in their behavior, . . . teaching what is good, that they may encourage the young women . . . that the word of God may not be dishonored. Likewise urge the young men to be sensible. (Titus 2:2–6)

Paul outlined the ideal situation: mature believers encouraging younger believers. Often nurturing doesn't happen, though, because we feel inadequate. Or sometimes we don't know how to start. Or we don't think we have the time.

You can start to overcome some of these concerns by following Paul and Barnabas' example from our lesson. The following questions should help you do this.

Do you know a younger Christian who is a new or immature believer? If you are an older man, write down the name of a younger man; if you are an older woman, a younger woman.

_____

What are this person's special needs at this time in life?

_____

_____

_____

From the lesson, we saw five ways in which Paul nurtured the young churches. How can you employ these methods in your younger friend's life?

• Strengthen their souls: _____

_____

• Encourage them to persevere: _____

_____

• Assist in organization: _____

_____

- Entrust them to the Lord: _____

_____

- Finish what they set out to accomplish: _____

_____

These can be the basic objectives for your nurturing relationship with a younger believer. The next Living Insight will help you plan more of the specifics.

✺ *Living Insights* STUDY TWO

You know who you want to nurture and what your overall goals are. Now let's explore how to bring them to life. When can you meet with this person?

_____

_____

In what ways can you build a relationship with this person other than your meeting times?

_____

_____

What skills do you wish to impart to this person? The following items may prod your thinking.

I'd like my friend to be able to:
- clearly communicate the gospel
- confront temptation
- make wise choices
- plan personal devotions

_____

_____

_____

Is there a curriculum you can use to help strengthen this young believer in the Scripture? If you don't know of any, call your local Christian bookstore or your pastor. Don't put off implementing this plan. Begin nurturing someone today.

Chapter 13

GRACE ON TRIAL

Acts 15:1–12

Not long after Christopher Columbus discovered the New World, the Reformers discovered—or rediscovered, we should say—the gospel. It had been hidden away for centuries in a damp dungeon of legalism. In those days, according to the religious higher-ups, human effort was the requirement for salvation. But when the Reformers heard the trapped cry of truth, they determined to set free the doctrine of salvation by faith alone. It was a valiant rescue, one filled with daring advances and vicious reprisals.

Trumpeting the cause the loudest was German monk Martin Luther. Of this fiery man, historian Philip Schaff wrote:

> Luther's writings smell of powder; his words are battles; he overwhelms his opponents with a roaring cannonade of argument, eloquence, passion, and abuse.[1]

He and his followers stood their ground against anyone who opposed the gospel of grace. And between their refusal to forsake reform and the church's refusal to abandon tradition, the smoke of church war billowed thick, and the guns of contention blazed red-hot.

However, Luther's friend and closest associate, Philipp Melanchthon, dreamed of the day when the battle fires would dim and the church would once again unite under truth's banner.

> Melanchthon was always ready for compromise and peace . . . and sincerely labored to restore the broken unity of the Church.[2]

> [He] declared that with tears as abundant as the waters of the river Elbe he could not express his grief over the distractions of Christendom and the "fury of theologians."[3]

1. Philip Schaff, *History of the Christian Church*, 2d ed., rev. (Grand Rapids, Mich.: William B. Eerdmans Publishing Co., 1910), vol. 7, p. 194.

2. Schaff, *History of the Christian Church*, p. 194.

3. Schaff, *History of the Christian Church*, p. 46.

His vision inspired Reformers throughout history, like English Puritan Richard Baxter, who distilled Melanchthon's desires into a timeless creed of Christian cooperation:

> In necessary things, unity; in doubtful things, liberty; in all things, charity.[4]

Like Luther, the apostle Paul also fought for grace. And like Melanchthon and Baxter, he longed for unity, liberty, and charity in the church. Let's observe how he achieves both ends when some of the Jewish Christian leaders in Jerusalem challenge the salvation of the Gentiles.

The Issue: Gentile Salvation

What's objectionable about Gentiles believing in Christ? Most of our churches today are made up of Gentiles. Why was this such an issue then?

To understand the situation, we must page back to the beginning of Acts and view the events in the book from the perspective of an average Jewish convert to Christianity.

Background Information

A Jew in that day might have reacted to Christ's last words before His ascension (Acts 1:8) like this:

Jesus: "You shall be My witnesses both in Jerusalem . . ."

Nate: "Great, let's go!"

Jesus: "and in all Judea . . ."

Nate: "Good idea, we have family in Judea."

Jesus: "and Samaria . . ."

Nate: "S-S-S-S-Samaria? We don't talk much to those half-breed Jews."

Jesus: "and even to the remotest part of the earth."

Nate: "Now wait just one minute! There are Gentiles out there!"

From childhood, Jews were taught to shun the "morally unclean" Gentiles. Even their culture was off-limits—Greek theater or sports, Roman fashions or music—all was forbidden.

The Jews who became Christians then carried this separatist attitude into their faith. It first surfaced when "a complaint arose

---

4. Richard Baxter, as quoted in *Bartlett's Familiar Quotations*, 15th ed., rev. and enl., ed. Emily Morison Beck (Boston, Mass.: Little, Brown and Co., 1980), p. 294.

on the part of the Hellenistic Jews against the native Hebrews, because their widows were being overlooked in the daily serving of food" (6:1b).

The Hellenists were Jews who had come to Palestine from other countries. Although they were Jewish by birth, they were Greek culturally—which the Jerusalem Jews perceived as contamination. So these Hellenists rightly felt that they were being discriminated against and that the native-born widows were being favored. Fortunately, this problem was wisely solved when the church leaders appointed impartial deacons to distribute the food. But this incident was just a taste of what was to come.

In a vision, Peter saw a sheetful of ceremonially unclean animals and heard a voice say, "Arise, Peter, kill and eat!" (10:13b). For kosher Peter, this idea was really hard to swallow. But the voice persisted, saying, "What God has cleansed, no longer consider unholy" (v. 15b). At first he was confused, but later it all made sense when he watched an "unclean" Gentile named Cornelius trust Christ and receive the Holy Spirit (vv. 44–48).

Peter had learned a lesson about grace: anyone can trust Christ and be saved. But the Jewish Christians back in Jerusalem, who hadn't had any such vision, struggled with the concept.

> When Peter came up to Jerusalem, those who were circumcised took issue with him, saying, "You went to uncircumcised men and ate with them." (11:2–3)

It was touch and go for awhile; but after Peter had explained God's hand in Cornelius' conversion, his Jewish-Christian brothers accepted his testimony and glorified God (vv. 4–18).

So the boiling issue had been contained thus far, but the lid blew sky-high once more when Paul and Barnabas returned from their first missionary journey and told of how God "had opened a door of faith to the Gentiles" (14:27b).

Internal Dissension

> And some men came down from Judea and began teaching the brethren, "Unless you are circumcised according to the custom of Moses, you cannot be saved." And . . . Paul and Barnabas had great dissension and debate with them. (15:1–2a)

When the Judean Jews, many of whom were former Pharisees,

heard these reports through the grapevine, they were troubled. Lloyd John Ogilvie helps us understand their struggle.

> For the Pharisee, a completed Jew, the Lord was the incarnate culmination of everything he had studied and learned. No need to do away with his heritage; now he was a fulfilled Hebrew among the still-expectant Hebrews. . . .
>
> But if Jesus was the Messiah of the Jews, what did he think about non-Hebrews who also became convinced of his Lordship? Now the Christian Pharisee had a problem. Conditioning and cultural pride flowed in his bloodstream. His people had paid a high price to maintain their uniqueness. He was not willing to give away the centuries of particularism that had made Israel a great people for the Lord to people who did not conform. If Jesus was the Hebrew Messiah, anyone wanting his salvation would have to become a Hebrew first! How else could he know the full meaning and purpose of God? . . . The Law of Moses must be maintained as the preliminary preparation to the new life in Christ. . . .
>
> . . . These converted Pharisees and their followers were not bad people; their problem was that they stood with one foot in Moses' Law and one foot in Christ's love. Now the ground was separating beneath them. They would have to leap one way or the other, but not without a frantic effort to hold back the earthquake and the resulting theological fault. Having tried to maintain "both-and," they were ending up with an "either-or" which contradicted the Messiah himself and his unqualified love for all.[5]

Surely, having been a Pharisee himself, Paul empathized with them; but that in no way lessened his distress at what they were teaching. They were tainting one of Christianity's essentials—God's pure and beautiful grace. So, in order to secure unity in the church, he had to fight.

5. Lloyd John Ogilvie, *Drumbeat of Love* (Waco, Tex.: Word Books, Publisher, 1976), pp. 191–92.

What Paul, Barnabas, and the church in Antioch did next was extremely critical. Their decision would affect the entire history of Christianity—and determine the way we view salvation today.

Wise Decision

Rather than pulling rank as apostles or ignoring the problem and hoping it would go away, Paul and Barnabas decided to discuss the issue openly and fairly. The church of Antioch also favored this approach, so

> the brethren determined that Paul and Barnabas and certain others of them should go up to Jerusalem to the apostles and elders concerning this issue. Therefore, being sent on their way by the church, they were passing through both Phoenicia and Samaria, describing in detail the conversion of the Gentiles, and were bringing great joy to all the brethren. (vv. 2b–3)

How did the Christians in these cities receive the news of Gentile salvation? With "great joy"! Notice, however, the contrasting response when Paul and Barnabas arrived in tradition-steeped Jerusalem.

> They were received by the church and the apostles and the elders, and they reported all that God had done with them. But certain ones of the sect of the Pharisees who had believed, stood up, saying, "It is necessary to circumcise them, and to direct them to observe the Law of Moses." (vv. 4a–5)

No warmth. No joy. Instead, rigidity chilled the air.

Interestingly, though traditionalism forced this issue, the early church displayed a remarkable openness in giving people the freedom to disagree. They didn't want to polarize Christ's church, but come to terms and have unity in the "necessary things."

> And the apostles and the elders came together to look into this matter. (v. 6)

The Investigation: Jerusalem Council

This meeting is known as the Jerusalem Council, and we can outline several positive steps the leaders made toward resolution and unity.

Statement of Purpose

First, they limited their agenda to one objective: determining the basis of Gentile salvation (called "this issue" in verse 2, "this matter" in verse 6). What resulted from this determination has impacted every generation since that day. If they had made a wrong decision, Christianity could have died away as a quasi-Jewish sect. Or the church could have split, weakening its influence. Or the gospel may not have ever traveled to Rome, Europe, and our ancestors.

Method of Discussion

The way they made their decision was as important as the decision itself. The unity of the church was at stake, so they had to show respect to both sides of the question. Consequently, they allowed "much debate" (v. 7a).

In our churches today, are we as open to differences of opinion? Are we gracious to those on the other side, willing to listen—really listen? In his letter to Timothy, Paul describes the attitude we should have when we discuss controversial matters:

> The Lord's bond-servant must not be quarrelsome,
> but be kind to all, able to teach, patient when wronged,
> with gentleness correcting those who are in opposi-
> tion, if perhaps God may grant them repentance lead-
> ing to the knowledge of the truth. (2 Tim. 2:24–25)

We can imagine that this was the atmosphere in the council room as the apostles and elders contended for the truth. But suddenly the debating stopped, and the room fell silent when Peter took the stand.

Testimony of Peter

Remembering Cornelius' salvation, Peter first spoke from personal experience.

> "Brethren, you know that in the early days God made
> a choice among you, that by my mouth the Gentiles
> should hear the word of the gospel and believe. And
> God, who knows the heart, bore witness to them,
> giving them the Holy Spirit, just as He also did to us;
> and He made no distinction between us and them,
> cleansing their hearts by faith." (Acts 15:7b–9)

Then, based on that experience, he asked a penetrating question that pointed out the main problem with the converted Pharisees' position: keeping the Law is humanly impossible.

> "Now therefore why do you put God to the test by placing upon the neck of the disciples a yoke which neither our fathers nor we have been able to bear?" (v. 10)

Finally, he clearly declared God's salvation for Jew or Gentile.

> "But we believe that we are saved through the grace of the Lord Jesus, in the same way as they also are." (v. 11)

God saves us by grace—regardless of our color, culture, social standing, or sex. We are all equal in Him.

Experiences of Paul and Barnabas

When Peter finished, Paul and Barnabas stood and enthusiastically described God's unbiased grace from their perspective.

> And all the multitude kept silent, and they were listening to Barnabas and Paul as they were relating what signs and wonders God had done through them among the Gentiles. (v. 12)

Those present began to sense a oneness as God threaded their hearts and minds together with the apostles' words. In our next lesson, we will see how grace fared at this trial, as the apostle James rises to speak for the elders at Jerusalem.

Some Timeless Principles

So far we can hear three voices of truth echoing through the council chambers.

First, *no conflict is ever easy.* Controversies are difficult to handle, and they require sensitivity and flexibility. When we debate with others, we must stay open to different opinions while holding fast to the truth we know. We must wisely distinguish what is essential and what is nonessential to the faith while maintaining unity and liberty. These are tough objectives; but once accomplished, they can bring lasting benefits.

As a result, *all conflict can be beneficial.* Disagreements can be good for a church. They sharpen our understanding of truth and chisel away traditions that dull our communication of the gospel. A church without questioning people loses its cutting edge in society and causes its members to become ineffective.

Third, *any kind of conflict calls for honest appraisal.* As a result of the Jerusalem Council, the Jewish Christians had to ask themselves some hard questions. "Do we really believe in God's grace? . . . Are we trusting Christ or our religion for salvation? . . . Why can't we accept the Gentiles? Could we be prejudiced? Self-centered? Arrogant?"

We must ask ourselves these same questions concerning our modern-day "Gentiles." Do we welcome into our fellowship those who look different than we do? Who talk differently? Whose pasts may be littered with failure or sin? Do we shun divorcées or single parents or rough-edged new converts? Are we willing to listen to others' opinions?

Do *we* really believe in God's grace?

⊙ *Living Insights* STUDY ONE

This chapter from Acts is not just about Gentile salvation—it's about being open to change.

The Jewish Christians knew only one way to relate to God— through the Law. But Christ changed all that. His death opened the gates of heaven so that anyone could enter in His name. This threatened the Hebrew believer, who enjoyed having an exclusive God. Like an only child who must now share a room with new siblings, the Jewish Christians struggled with this change.

How do you take to change? Are you flexible when grace makes changes in your own law? Examine your attitudes toward change by circling the appropriate number under each item in the following list.

- The church leaders want to change the style of worship to make non-Christians feel more comfortable.

I'd be resistant.   I'd be flexible.

1   2   3   4   5

- You enjoy hosting an annual neighborhood barbecue at your house. This year your spouse wants to invite a new family who is from another culture and speaks little English.

I'd be resistant.   I'd be flexible.

1   2   3   4   5

- You have teenage children and enjoy having the youth group over to your house on Sunday nights. The youth pastor wants to start bringing some rougher, non-Christian teenagers to the group.

I'd be resistant.   I'd be flexible.

1   2   3   4   5

God's grace always challenges us to be open to any change that better communicates the gospel. In fact, God is probably gently pushing a grace change in your life right now. If so, write down what it is.

_____

_____

_____

Have you been resistant to this change? What do you need to do to be more flexible?

_____

_____

_____

✸ *Living Insights* _____ STUDY TWO

Like a grindstone, conflict handled properly can sharpen us. Are sparks flying in one of your relationships right now? If so, describe the conflict.

_____

_____

_____

_____

Recall for a moment Baxter's words: "In necessary things, unity; in doubtful things, liberty; in all things, charity." Does your disagreement center on a necessary thing or a secondary issue? Is it truly worth fighting for?

_____

_____

"In all things," are you holding to "charity" as your goal and motivation? What is going on in the depths of your heart?

_____

_____

_____

Thinking back on how Paul and Barnabas handled their conflict with the Jewish Christians, in what ways can you exhibit the same openness and fairness in your conflict?

_____

_____

How do you think this conflict is sharpening you?

_____

_____

_____

Now thank the Lord for your conflicts. It may be His way of honing the rough edges in your life and sharpening you to serve Him better.

Chapter 14
THE ESSENTIALS
Acts 15:13–35

D on't forget—*fundamentals!*"

From Little League to the pros, all coaches emphasize this watchword. They know that the key to winning is performing the fundamentals of the game.

During the 1960s, legendary football coach Vince Lombardi led his Green Bay Packers to a record three consecutive championships by honing and polishing the fundamentals. He drilled and drilled his players in the rudiments of blocking, tackling, and running. Biographer Michael O'Brien comments:

> Vince's strategy was not particularly creative. Seldom dazzling, his teams concentrated on vigorous, quick, synchronized execution of the fundamental elements of football. He did what everybody else did, only he did it better.[1]

On one occasion, so the story goes, his team neglected the fundamentals and lost to an inferior squad. The next practice, Lombardi soberly addressed the sheepish athletes: "OK, we go back to the basics this morning. Gentlemen, *this* is a *football!*"[2]

You can't get more basic than that! Sometimes we, too, forget the fundamentals—not in sports but in the Christian life. And we, too, need to go back to the basics. The first group of Christians to do this in an official way was the Jerusalem Council. They met to define the essentials of salvation[3]—the most important fundamental of them all.

---

1. Michael O'Brien, *Vince: A Personal Biography of Vince Lombardi* (New York, N.Y.: William Morrow and Co., 1987), p. 238.

2. As told by Charles R. Swindoll in *Growing Strong in the Seasons of Life* (Portland, Oreg.: Multnomah Press, 1983), p. 373.

3. The word *essentials* appears in Acts 15:28: "For it seemed good to the Holy Spirit and to us to lay upon you no greater burden than these essentials." In Greek, the word means, "it is compulsory, necessary." See G. Abbott-Smith, *A Manual Greek Lexicon of the New Testament*, 3d ed. (Edinburgh, Scotland: T. and T. Clark, 1937), p. 164.

A Review of the Disagreement

In our previous lesson, we saw that the central question of debate between the apostles and elders was, What should a Gentile do to be saved? Certain Jewish Christians, former Pharisees, felt that the Gentiles must keep the Law in order to be saved. "It is necessary," they insisted, "to circumcise them, and to direct them to observe the Law of Moses" (Acts 15:5b).

But Peter objected. How could Gentiles be expected to obey the Law when even the Jews hadn't been able to keep it (v. 10)? So he concluded,

> "We believe that we are saved through the grace of the Lord Jesus, in the same way as they also are." (v. 11)

Fundamentally, salvation comes by faith in Christ plus . . . nothing else. The essential ingredient in salvation is grace, not law. Paul and Barnabas affirmed Peter's statement with delight, giving example upon example of God's grace in action through them (v. 12). When they finished speaking, all eyes turned to the council members. As in a courtroom, both sides had rested their cases; now it was time to make the decision.

A Solution to the Disagreement

James, the half brother of Jesus and the writer of the epistle bearing his name, rose and spoke for the council. A respected Christian with high integrity, he communicated the decision logically, clearly, and compassionately.

An Oral Decision

"Brethren, listen to me," James began (v. 13b). Then using four strands of thought, he wove a wise doctrinal pattern for the church to follow.

First, he said that God is doing this, not man. This point had been clearly made by Peter, or Simeon, as James called him by his Hebrew name.

> "Simeon has related how God first concerned Himself about taking from among the Gentiles a people for His name." (v. 14)

The Jewish Christians thought they had God figured out. They knew Him as a God of law. Who was this new God of grace? And how could the God who loved the Jew have any room for the Gentile?

But James was reminding them that they couldn't fashion God from their own preconceptions and force that image on others; God's ways are often incomprehensible. And now, by His grace He was bringing Gentiles into His family without all the Jewish trappings. This, as James explained in his next point, had been God's plan all along.

Referring to a prophecy by Amos, James threaded a second strand into his presentation: *the Word of God is being fulfilled, not contradicted.*

> "And with this the words of the Prophets agree, just
>   as it is written,
>   'After these things I will return,
>   And I will rebuild the tabernacle of David
>   which has fallen,
>   And I will rebuild its ruins,
>   And I will restore it,
>   In order that the rest of mankind may
>   seek the Lord,
>   And all the Gentiles who are called by My
>   name,'
>   Says the Lord, who makes these things
>   known from of old."
>   (vv. 15–18)

In verse 16, "after these things" refers to the time after the church age—which is like a parenthesis in God's plan for the Jews.

In the Old Testament, God selected the Jews to be His people, promising to bless them as a nation. When they rejected Christ, God temporarily rejected them while raising His church (see Rom. 11:25). At the appointed time, Christ will return, rebuild the temple, and restore the Jews to Himself, finally fulfilling all His promises to them.

The following chart illustrates how the church age fits into that plan.[4]

---

4. Adapted from a chart by Irving L. Jensen, in *Jensen Bible Study Charts* (Chicago, Ill.: Moody Press, 1976), vol. 1, chart 24.

Israel in Relation to the Church Age

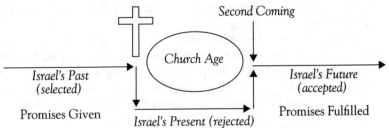

By quoting Amos' prophecy, James was showing the Jewish Christians that Gentile salvation was part of God's plan. This conclusion formulated the third strand of his argument: *the basis of salvation is grace, not law.*

> "Therefore it is my judgment that we do not trouble those who are turning to God from among the Gentiles." (Acts 15:19)

James declared that the Jewish believers should not burden the Gentile Christians by requiring that they keep the Law. God had already saved them; to add their own requirements would be opposing God's grace and bringing great "trouble" to fellow believers.

Completing his theological pattern for the church, James adds a cautionary fourth strand: *a lifestyle of obedience and love must follow salvation, not license.*

> "But that we write to them that they abstain from things contaminated by idols and from fornication and from what is strangled and from blood. For Moses from ancient generations has in every city those who preach him, since he is read in the synagogues every Sabbath." (vv. 20–21)

Was James qualifying all he had said about grace? Far from it. He was just foreseeing an oil-and-water problem occurring as more and more Gentiles began mixing with Jews in the newly founded churches.

Jewish Christians had been raised under a strict moral and dietary code. Among the most heinous offenses were the four that James mentioned: fornication, eating meat from animals offered to idols, eating meat from strangled animals, and eating meat with blood in it (see Lev. 17:10–16; 18:6–30). The Gentile believers, however, had no such restraints. So conflict between the two groups was inevitable.

Wishing to avoid needless and often unintentional offense, James wanted to remind the Gentile Christians to love their Jewish brothers and sisters by voluntarily restricting their liberty in these kinds of practices. "Don't flaunt your freedom," James was saying. Later, Paul echoed this same message to the Galatian churches:

> For you were called to freedom, brethren; only do not turn your freedom into an opportunity for the flesh, but through love serve one another. (Gal. 5:13)

God's grace has delivered us from legalism, but that doesn't give us license to do anything we please. Limiting our freedom for the sake of others shows maturity—the kind of maturity James wanted to instill in the quickly multiplying Gentile believers.

A Written Statement

The council agreed with James and recorded their decision in the following letter.

> "The apostles and the brethren who are elders, to the brethren in Antioch and Syria and Cilicia who are from the Gentiles, greetings. Since we have heard that some of our number to whom we gave no instruction have disturbed you with their words, un-settling your souls, it seemed good to us, having be-come of one mind, to select men to send to you with our beloved Barnabas and Paul, men who have risked their lives for the name of our Lord Jesus Christ. Therefore we have sent Judas and Silas, who them-selves will also report the same things by word of mouth. For it seemed good to the Holy Spirit and to us to lay upon you no greater burden than these essentials: that you abstain from things sacrificed to idols and from blood and from things strangled and from fornication; if you keep yourselves free from such things, you will do well. Farewell." (Acts 15:23b–29)

Two points stand out in this brief correspondence. First, the council members recognize that *restricting one's liberty is a burden.*

When they write "it seemed good to us . . . to lay upon you no greater burden," by implication they *are* laying on them some amount of burden.

Limitations are burdensome. But love motivates us to bear them to protect weaker believers from stumbling.

Second, *these restrictions are essential.* The council members called the limitations "essentials" because the church couldn't win without them. Harmony in the body of Christ often depends on our willingness to forego a privilege. This is not capitulating to legalism; it is a sign of love and maturity.

A Public Announcement

Letter in hand, Paul, Barnabas, Judas, and Silas traveled to Antioch

> and having gathered the congregation together, they delivered the letter. And when they had read it, they rejoiced because of its encouragement. And Judas and Silas, also being prophets themselves, encouraged and strengthened the brethren with a lengthy message. And after they had spent time there, they were sent away from the brethren in peace to those who had sent them out. But it seemed good to Silas to remain there. But Paul and Barnabas stayed in Antioch, teaching and preaching, with many others also, the word of the Lord. (vv. 30b–35)

The response to the council's decision was tremendous! The people rejoiced, were encouraged and strengthened; they felt a sense of peace and continued preaching the Word as one voice.

The Jerusalem Council's emphasis on grace and love averted a serious schism. So for now, there was harmony. But down the road, the apostles would battle additional opponents of grace. One was legalism—the teaching that salvation is earned by following a list of do's and don'ts. The opposite extreme was the philosophy of total freedom from any law. Then there was another twist—the fallacy propagated in the Galatian churches that salvation is by grace, but spirituality is measured by the Law.[5]

5. The book of Romans was written to confront legalism; James was written to oppose total license, called *antinomianism*; and Galatians was written to straighten out those who determined how spiritual they were by how well they kept the Law, a philosophy aptly called *Galatianism.*

We face these same opponents today, don't we? If we are to win, we must focus on the fundamentals: God's grace, salvation through faith alone, freedom in Christ, and making loving sacrifices for one another.

A Response to the Solution

We tend to complicate these simple essentials, swinging the pendulum of God's grace from legalism to license. Each extreme has its negative consequences: legalism results in an emphasis on works, and the impact is guilt; while license results in an emphasis on self, and the impact is offense. One says, "If you don't achieve, you're a failure"; the other says, "Do it your way, and don't worry about others' feelings."

In the middle is grace. Grace results in an emphasis on Christ, and the impact is love. It says, "Love others as Christ has loved you." This is the essence of the Christian life. And like so many coaches all over the world, our heavenly Coach will keep on reminding us, "Don't forget—*fundamentals!*" Will we listen?

 Living Insights STUDY ONE

You receive an end-of-the-month paycheck—that's not grace. You give your son an allowance for doing his chores—that's not grace either. You return a favor by baby-sitting your neighbor's kids—no grace here. Where can we find grace?

Grace is the prodigal son returning home to a party in his honor or Jesus spying a wicked little man in a sycamore tree and saying, "Zaccheus, . . . today I must stay at your house" (Luke 19:5b). Grace is Jesus saying to the thief who languishes on the cross next to His: "Today you shall be with Me in Paradise" (23:43).

Why is the first set of examples not grace, while the second set is? For clues, read Romans 4:4–5 and 11:6.

_____

_____

In your own words, write out a definition for grace. If you need a model, try Ephesians 2:4–9.

_____

Why do you think grace is a fundamental of Christianity?

_____

_____

Where are some places you have found grace in your life? What are some ways you can express grace to those within your reach?

_____

_____

_____

_____

 ## *Living Insights*

Another essential of grace-filled Christianity we discovered in our lesson is love—love that is willing to limit one's own freedom to protect a weaker fellow Christian.[6] "But how is one to know," asks Charles Ryrie candidly,

> if something is a genuine hindrance or whether the person who objects to your doing something is simply trying to impose his Christian standard on you?[7]

Our principle of love can degenerate into checklist Christianity. We don't want to offend this group of people, so we keep their list of right and wrong. Neither do we want to offend that group, so we follow their standard as well. Soon these lists constrict us like strips of cloth on a mummy. We can feel entombed, restrained, and even afraid of pleasure.

Ryrie proposes two guidelines to help us unwrap this dilemma and know when and where not to limit our freedom.

---

6. Paul expands this principle in Romans 14 and 1 Corinthians 8.

7. Charles Caldwell Ryrie, *Balancing the Christian Life* (Chicago, Ill.: Moody Press, 1969), p. 156.

[1] Is the objecting person really trying to grow and make progress in his own spiritual life, or is he simply sitting on the sidelines of the racecourse sniping at the runners? . . . [2] How many are apparently affected by what I may feel free to do?[8]

To bring this into the realm of the personal, suppose your friend is battling overeating. You would probably restrict your freedom to eat doughnuts in front of this person in order to protect your friend from stumbling. In addition, let's say you decide to minister to a group of people like your friend. Because of the number of people affected, you may completely alter your diet to be an example for them. You do this because you love them.

However, suppose a group of your friends is critical of anyone who eats sugar. Doughnut-eaters offend them, not because they are in danger of stumbling, but because—in pride—they enjoy announcing that their way is better. These people are merely "sniping at the runners."[9]

In the following space, evaluate one of your freedoms. Maybe you have been limiting yourself unnecessarily, or maybe you need to begin restricting this privilege because someone else is truly stumbling. Write down the freedom, use Ryrie's guidelines to determine whether to limit it, then express your commitment to do what is most loving.

_____

_____

_____

_____

_____

_____

_____

8. Ryrie, *Balancing the Christian Life*, p. 157.

9. Paul expressed the godly attitudes that people on either side of a controversial practice should have: "Let not him who eats regard with contempt him who does not eat, and let not him who does not eat judge him who eats, for God has accepted him" (Rom. 14:3).

Chapter 15
WHEN COWORKERS CLASH
Acts 15:36–41

The Bible never flatters its heroes. One moment we read about David bravely slinging a stone at Goliath, the next we see him casting a lustful glance at Bathsheba. We admire Peter when he leaves his nets to follow Jesus, but we shake our heads when he denies Him on the eve of His crucifixion.

Scripture paints its characters realistically . . . and that is good news. We can identify with these people in the Bible. They're just like us; and if God can use them, He can use us too.

At the end of Acts 15, historian Luke displays Paul and Barnabas in realism's unflinching light. These two missionaries weren't plaster saints. They were fallible men who had headstrong opinions—opinions that sometimes clashed. In the following passage, such a clash of wills occurs between them that they end up parting ways, never to minister together again.

Have you had a similar stomach-churning confrontation? Most everyone has. It is our hope that in looking at Paul and Barnabas' dissonant clash we will learn a few lessons about preserving harmony while disagreeing.

Some Facts about Disagreement

As we begin our study, it will be helpful to remember these four truths about disagreements.

First, *disagreements are inevitable.* Like fingerprints, each person's background, temperament, and set of opinions are unique; different from anyone else's. And because of these differences, people will naturally disagree with one another. This isn't a bad thing—it's just part of being human.

Second, *even godly people will not always agree.* Disagreeing is not necessarily a sign of carnality. By accommodating one another in love, mature believers can disagree without being disagreeable. Robert Cook's healthy attitude exemplifies this fact: "God reserves the right to use people who disagree with me."[1]

---

1. Robert A. Cook in *Quote Unquote*, comp. Lloyd Cory (Wheaton, Ill.: Scripture Press Publications, Victor Books, 1977), p. 87.

Third, *every disagreement has the same two ingredients: an issue and varying viewpoints.* The issue always involves principles; the viewpoints always involve personalities. Differing points of view on the same issue are what usually make for conflict, not two different issues. Simply identifying the issue and the viewpoints can greatly help us understand one another and move us toward a resolution.

Fourth, *in many disagreements, each side is valid.* In the heated fray of an argument, we usually see only one side—our own. If we calm down, though, we can begin to see the issue from the other side. And if we're honest, we'll have to admit that the conflict is really a matter of perspective rather than who's right and who's wrong. Each side has valid points.

The clash between Barnabas and Paul clearly illustrates all four of these facts, so let's examine their disagreement, beginning with some background information.

A Case Study: Paul and Barnabas

Their argument springs from the well of trouble they encountered on their first missionary journey. Probably the capper was when their assistant on that trip, John Mark, deserted them in Pamphylia (see Acts 13:5, 13). We're not sure why he abandoned ship. Perhaps seeing Paul fall sick in Perga discouraged him, or maybe he feared for his own life. He might have disagreed with Paul's leadership or the new emphasis on Gentile salvation. Whatever his reason for leaving, the point is that he let them down.

Later, Paul wants to embark on a second missionary journey.

> Paul said to Barnabas, "Let us return and visit the brethren in every city in which we proclaimed the word of the Lord, and see how they are." (15:36)

The idea sounds good to Barnabas, so they begin making plans. They could try a new route over land instead of by sea; they could share the letter from the Jerusalem Council with the Gentile converts; they could encourage and strengthen all the new believers as well as old friends in the Lord. But before they even pull their suitcases down from the attic, they hit a snag concerning John Mark that jeopardizes the entire mission.

The Issue

As Paul and Barnabas sit down to discuss the details, we can imagine their conversation. Barnabas says, "I'll get the maps and buy our tickets."

"Okay," says Paul. "I'll send word ahead to let them know we're coming."

"And I'll tell John Mark to start packing. Just think, it'll be the three of us again—this is gonna be great!"

Paul drops his quill and stares at Barnabas. "John Mark? *He's* not coming. No sir! Not John Mark!"

At the heart of their disagreement is this issue: Should someone who defected be given a second chance? Barnabas says yes; Paul says no. Let's step into the minds of these men and see the issue from each of their perspectives.

The Viewpoints

Luke first shines a light on Barnabas' thinking.

> Barnabas was desirous of taking John, called Mark, along with them also. (v. 37)

The phrase "was desirous" does little justice to the original Greek tense. The verb means "to will, to want, to wish," which is strong in itself, but Luke uses the imperfect tense, emphasizing Barnabas' tenacity.[2] He *continually* desired to take John Mark—his feet were firmly planted, and he was standing his ground on this issue.

Barnabas is thinking, John Mark needs encouragement. He needs another chance. Sure, John Mark blew it, but don't we all? God can still use him.

> But Paul kept insisting that they should not take him along who had deserted them in Pamphylia and had not gone with them to the work. (v. 38)

Matching the intensity of Barnabas' opinion is Paul's viewpoint. Luke again uses the imperfect tense, "kept insisting," to describe the Apostle's approach. To Paul, young John Mark was unreliable. When you're going into battle, you need someone who won't break under fire. Perhaps Paul had in mind the proverb,

> Putting confidence in an unreliable man is like chewing with a sore tooth, or trying to run on a broken foot. (Prov. 25:19 TLB)

---

2. Fritz Rienecker, *A Linguistic Key to the Greek New Testament* (Grand Rapids, Mich.: Zondervan Publishing House, Regency Reference Library, 1980), p. 300.

Our practical side may go with Paul, but our hearts side with Barnabas. After all, God even gave Paul himself, who was a persecutor of the church, a second chance (see 1 Tim. 1:12–15). We can say this about almost every Bible character: Moses, Rahab, Jonah, and Peter. We can even add ourselves to the list. But Paul had a different perspective, making these two men a real study in contrasts.

> Barnabas was people-oriented; Paul was more task-oriented. Barnabas was a man of compassion; Paul was a man of conviction. Barnabas was a builder of men; Paul was a planter of churches.
>
> Paul looked at the issue from the viewpoint of the overall good of the ministry. Barnabas looked at the issue from the viewpoint of the overall good of the man.[3]

Is one perspective right and the other wrong? Since the issue doesn't involve essential doctrine, we can genuinely say both sides are right. There are good arguments for both sides of this issue, and our goal is not to be swayed to one side or the other. We merely want to be impressed with the value of examining both viewpoints in order to arrive at a good solution.

The Solution

Unfortunately, of the solutions available to Barnabas and Paul, they choose the saddest: separation.

> There arose such a sharp disagreement that they separated from one another,[4] and Barnabas took Mark with him and sailed away to Cyprus. But Paul chose Silas and departed. (Acts 15:39–40a)

Stalemated, the two friends and brothers in Christ lose something precious to both of them: the other's presence. A. T. Robertson

---

3. See the study guide *The Grace Awakening*, coauthored by Ken Gire, from the Bible-teaching ministry of Charles R. Swindoll (Fullerton, Calif.: Insight for Living, 1990), p. 81.

4. Luke expresses the tragedy of the situation by using the Greek word *paroxysm*, translated "sharp disagreement." "Interestingly, our English word 'paroxysm' is transliterated letter for letter. Webster says *paroxysm* is 'a fit, attack, or sudden increase or recurrence of symptoms (as of a disease).' It is a convulsion, a violent emotion. Such a rift resulted from Paul and Barnabas' disagreement that the torn relationship could not be easily or quickly mended." Gire, *The Grace Awakening* study guide, pp. 81–82.

recognized what each missionary forfeited by leaving the other.

> Paul and Barnabas parted in anger and both in sorrow. Paul owed more to Barnabas than to any other man. Barnabas was leaving the greatest spirit of the time and of all times.[5]

So with the disagreement unresolved, Barnabas sails out of Paul's life. Never again is the "son of encouragement" mentioned in Acts, his name only appearing a few times in the rest of the New Testament.[6] However, every time we read Mark's gospel, we taste the fruit of Barnabas' ministry in the life of that young man—he became a biographer of Jesus and eventually even won Paul's respect (see Col. 4:10; 2 Tim. 4:11; Philem. 23–24).

The Departure

While Barnabas and John Mark sailed off to Cyprus, Paul

> chose Silas and departed, being committed by the brethren to the grace of the Lord. And he was traveling through Syria and Cilicia, strengthening the churches. (Acts 15:40–41)

The Greek word for *committed* combines two words: *beside*, and *give* or *supply*. With Barnabas out of the picture, the church committed Paul and Silas to the Lord, supplying them with the necessities for their trip. Paul may have won the argument in the eyes of the church, but he had lost a friend.

Some Things We Have Learned

Paul and Barnabas' tragic breach reminds us how tenuous even the closest relationships can be. It was Barnabas who defended young convert Saul in Jerusalem, searched for him in Tarsus, and dabbed his wounds in Lystra. He was his mentor, his encourager, his supporter. Now the ties were broken, and the memories shelved away like a forgotten photo album.

To avoid this kind of tragedy in your relationships, attach the

---

5. Archibald Thomas Robertson, *Word Pictures in the New Testament* (Grand Rapids, Mich.: Baker Book House, 1930), vol. 3, p. 241.

6. Paul refers to Barnabas in three of his letters—in 1 Corinthians 9:6; Galatians 2:1, 9, 13; and Colossians 4:10.

following three reminders like magnets to your thoughts when disagreements arise.

First, *work hard at seeing both viewpoints*. This is indeed hard work, because it's not natural. Our pride is at stake when someone disagrees with us. As a result, we can become myopic, seeing only our own position while blurring everyone else's. When this happens, we need a few eye drops of objectivity, honesty, and humility to clear up our vision. As Paul himself prescribed:

> Do nothing from selfishness or empty conceit, but with humility of mind let each of you regard one another as more important than himself; do not merely look out for your own personal interests, but also for the interests of others. (Phil. 2:3–4)

Looking out for the interests of others means that we identify with their feelings; we open our eyes to their position, being willing to say, "I see your point."

Second, *when both sides have good support, seek a wise compromise*. Paul and Barnabas didn't have to split up. Does that surprise you? They could have compromised by choosing one of the options suggested by Leslie Flynn.

> Could Paul have said, "We'll tell him he's on probation. If he doesn't work out the first month, we'll ship him home again." . . .
>
> Or perhaps Barnabas could have conceded, "We do need dedicated workers on our team. Let's give Mark a minor assignment to see how he does. Meanwhile we'll start on our journey and, if we hear he's measuring up, we'll send for him to join us along the way." . . .
>
> Or could they have agreed on a contingent plan? "Let's take Mark, but others also. If Mark deserts us again, we'll have others to fall back on." Either the inventiveness of love should have discovered some middle ground, or the submission of love should have yielded the point entirely.[7]

7. Leslie B. Flynn, *When the Saints Come Storming In* (Wheaton, Ill.: Scripture Press Publications, Victor Books, 1988), p. 67.

Who knows what creative alternative to separation they could have agreed upon? In our disagreements, we, too, may have a rack full of compromise options from which to choose. We just have to be willing to find the one that fits best.

Third, *if the conflict persists, care enough to work it through*. Don't run from conflict. Don't quit your job, your church, or your marriage because of disagreements. Slamming down the phone or slamming shut the door doesn't help matters, and neither does resorting to the silent treatment. Truly caring about a relationship means you're willing to face the issue and, with God's help, work it out in love.

 Living Insights

How do you view conflicts? David Augsburger has noted four different perspectives on conflict that can help us determine our own.

> If I view conflict as a fixed matter of fate, explaining, "We just can't get along—we're incompatible—we'll never understand each other—that's all there is to it," then my life pattern will be one of avoiding threat and going my own safe, secure, well-armored way.
>
> If I see conflict as crushing, "If we clash, I'll be judged—I'll be rejected—our friendship will fall through," then my life pattern will be acting the nice guy, quickly giving in to keep things comfortable.
>
> If I view conflict as an inevitable matter of right and wrong, "I owe it to you, to me, to others, to God, to defend my truth and show you your error," my life will be rigid, perhaps perfectionistic, and judgmental.
>
> If I see conflict as natural, neutral, normal, I may be able to see the difficulties we experience as tensions in relationships and honest differences in perspective that can be worked through by caring about each other and each confronting the other with truth expressed by love.[8]

---

8. David Augsburger, *Caring Enough to Confront* (Glendale, Calif.: G/L Publications, Regal Books, 1973), pp. 3–4.

Which one of Augsburger's scenarios describes your perspective most of the time?

❏ Conflict is a matter of fate. ❏ Conflict is a matter of right and wrong.

❏ Conflict is always crushing. ❏ Conflict is neutral and normal.

Describe a recent conflict you had with a friend or family member. How did your perspective influence the way you handled the confrontation?

_____

_____

_____

_____

Perhaps you wish you had handled it differently. Maybe you didn't approach this disagreement as an honest difference in viewpoint "that can be worked through by caring about each other and each confronting the other with truth expressed by love." If so, how can you bind up any wounded feelings?

_____

_____

_____

_____

Paul and Barnabas parted ways, never to cross paths again. If you can, don't let your recent disagreement separate you and your friend or family member. A few moments of heated argument are not worth a lifetime of regret.

⊛ *Living Insights*

For many of us, disagreements come and go as often as airplanes at a big-city airport. If a conflict is on the taxiway in your life right now, the three applications from the lesson can guide it to the runway and out of your relationship.

- Work hard at seeing both viewpoints. With honesty, objectivity, and humility, write down both viewpoints in your present disagreement.

_____

_____

_____

- Seek a wise compromise. What compromise options are available to you?

_____

_____

_____

- Care enough to work through the disagreement, rather than run. What will it take to work it through?

_____

_____

_____

Chapter 16

WHAT OPENS WHEN DOORS CLOSE?

Acts 15:41–16:10

H as this ever happened to your family? Dad loads up the minivan with all the vacation necessities: suitcases and sunscreen, fishing poles and lucky lures, tennis rackets, bicycles, an ice chest, and a stack of full-color touring guides. Soon everyone piles aboard, and Dad steers the family-mobile onto the open road.

Hours later, after ten rounds of "Found a Peanut" and as many bathroom breaks, your family finally arrives at the well-manicured hotel that you have picked out from *Vacation Monthly*, page 2.

Suddenly, Dad stops the van, and there's a collective groan. Glowing in red neon in the front window are the disheartening words, No Vacancy.

So your family tries the hotel on page 32—No Vacancy. The one on page 55—No Vacancy. Page 93—No Vacancy. Even the last page, Motel Bear Claw . . . still No Vacancy.

Everywhere you turn, closed doors confront you.

Closed doors aren't limited to family vacations, however. They have a way of popping up in all areas of your life. Expectantly, you set out for some grand goal. The road is smooth and the timing seems right, then, without warning—slam. One door closes, then another, and another.

That's Paul's situation in his second missionary journey—a journey that began with high hopes for evangelizing Asia and almost ended with a string of closed doors and No Vacancy signs.

Prepared for the Second Journey

Paul had every reason to expect that his second journey would be as successful as his first. Remember the report he gave in Antioch after he and Barnabas returned from Pamphylia?

> When they had arrived and gathered the church together, they began to report all things that God had done with them and how He had opened a door of faith to the Gentiles. (Acts 14:27)

Logged in his memory was God's power among the Gentiles. Surely, God would hold this door of faith open on his second trip as well.

In addition, the Jerusalem Council had recently laid the doctrinal foundation for Gentile salvation (15:6–29). He had found a new traveling partner, one with enthusiasm and energy (v. 40a). And the Antioch church was fully supporting and encouraging him (v. 40b). All these factors flowed together like tributaries, forming a bubbling river of excitement for the journey ahead.

Blessing in Familiar Territory

Choosing a land rather than a sea route to Asia, Paul and Silas hike to Tarsus, Paul's hometown, through a pass called the Cilician Gates, and up into the Taurus Mountains. This is familiar territory for Paul, a welcome sight as he walks along, savoring the anticipation of reunion with his Asian friends.

Strengthening the Churches

When he finally reaches them, the doors are wide open for him to accomplish his first objective: to strengthen the churches (v. 41). Luke records no persecution in this area where Paul previously suffered such abuse. Instead, he and Silas are free to teach and encourage the Christians.

Choosing Timothy

When they come to Derbe and then Lystra, one of Paul's young converts, Timothy, impresses them with his rapid growth in Christ. Here is the first mention of this man who would become Paul's protégé and one of the early church's

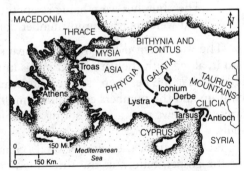

The Second Journey Begins[1]

1. *Life Application® Bible*, New International Version (copublishers; Wheaton, Ill.: Tyndale House Publishers, 1991 and Grand Rapids, Mich.: Zondervan Publishing House, 1991), p. 1990. Maps © 1986, 1988 by Tyndale House Publishers, Inc. All rights reserved. Used by permission.

first pastors (see 1 Tim. 1:1–2; 4:14; 2 Tim. 1:1–6).

> Behold, a certain disciple was there, named Timothy,
> the son of a Jewish woman who was a believer, but
> his father was a Greek, and he was well spoken of
> by the brethren who were in Lystra and Iconium.
> Paul wanted this man to go with him; and he took
> him and circumcised him because of the Jews who
> were in those parts, for they all knew that his father
> was a Greek. (Acts 16:1b–3)

What the Apostle had seen lacking in John Mark, he found in Timothy, who had a good reputation among the believers in the area and was willing to stay by his side on the road. This was another open door for Paul—he longed to groom a younger man to carry on the ministry, and Timothy was the perfect choice.[2]

Delivering Decrees

With Timothy now aboard, the missionaries travel throughout the region explaining the decree from the Jerusalem Council (v. 4). This shows yet another open door in their ministry, for the people's response is positive. In fact, Luke records encouraging, phenomenal growth in every church.

Experiencing Growth

> The churches were being strengthened in the faith,
> and were increasing in number daily. (v. 5)

The word *strengthened* in Greek means "to make firm or solid," and it, along with the verb *increasing*, is in the imperfect tense. This tells us that the believers' spiritual muscles were continually being built up and the numbers continually multiplying. For the missionaries, this news puts a fresh spring in their step and a fire in their souls.

At every turn, the wind of God's Spirit is pushing doors open for the gospel. Surely, as the three men venture further into Asia, God will whisk them through more open doors to even greater

---

2. Because Timothy is half-Jewish—his mother is a Jewish believer, but his father is Greek—Paul circumcises him to remove any barriers to the gospel. Now the Jews could not say, "We're not interested" because of Timothy, and the new Jewish believers would not be turned off to Timothy as a pastor in training.

successes! Hearts pounding with anticipation, they head into the surrounding regions. Suddenly, though, the wind stops.

Blocked from New Regions

In Revelation 3:7b–8a, John records Jesus' words to the church in ancient Philadelphia—words that may be unfamiliar and surprising to many:

> "He who is holy, who is true, who has the key of David, who opens and no one will shut, and who shuts and no one opens, says this: 'I know your deeds. Behold, I have put before you an open door which no one can shut.'"

Because of the Philadelphia church's reverence and commitment, Christ opened wide a door of ministry and growth for them. However, just as He opens some doors, He also closes others—"who shuts and no one can open." We are more used to thinking of God as a door opener, not the door closer, aren't we? But He does both, as we see from what happens to Paul's ministry as he travels deeper into Asia.

Forbidden to Speak

> And they passed through the Phrygian and Galatian region, having been forbidden by the Holy Spirit to speak the word in Asia. (Acts 16:6)

The word *forbidden* in Greek is derived from *kolos*, an older word that means "to cut short," "to lop" or "to trim."[3] In a sense, the missionaries forged ahead in one direction, and the Holy Spirit cut them off. They went another way; they were cut off again. Like mice in a maze, they wandered from here to there, not able to settle or minister anywhere in Phrygia or Galatia.

Kept from Entering

Eventually, they arrive at the outskirts of the next province.

> And when they had come to Mysia, they were trying to go into Bithynia, and the Spirit of Jesus did not

---

3. Gerhard Kittel, ed., *Theological Dictionary of the New Testament*, trans. and ed., Geoffrey W. Bromiley (Grand Rapids, Mich.: William B. Eerdmans Publishing Co., 1965), vol. 3, p. 814.

permit them; and passing by Mysia, they came down
to Troas. (vv. 7–8)

More closed doors! Try as they may, God was blocking their
efforts. Was it for lack of needy people in these regions? On the
contrary, these men and women needed Christ too. Even so, Christ
was restraining His messengers and His message.

Likewise, in our lives, God will sometimes shut down an exciting
ministry or allow obstacles in our paths like sickness, financial difficulties, job failure, or a relationship breakup. At times like these,
it's easy to become frustrated and disheartened. We can't imagine
why God would shut some of the doors that He does. So we try to
explain it, saying, "Maybe we just made a mistake . . . maybe we
need to try harder." But when Christ closes a door, He merely has
His sights on something better—something around the bend we
can't see yet. For Paul, that something was Europe.

Directed to Another Plan

Paul had planned to evangelize Asia, but for now, Asia was
merely God's hallway for His men to pass through. Along the way
they jiggled doorknobs and tested locks, but no doors opened . . .
until they reached the very end of the corridor.

A Vision

Passing through Mysia, Paul and his companions finally arrive
in Troas, a city on the western edge of Asia that overlooks the
Aegean Sea (v. 8). God has blocked them from going north, south,
or east; so here they stand with their toes in the sand, at Asia's
westernmost point. Who would they witness to here? The fish?

There's nothing to do, except wait on God and get some rest.
While they sleep,

> a vision appeared to Paul in the night: a certain man
> of Macedonia was standing and appealing to him, and
> saying, "Come over to Macedonia and help us." (v. 9)

"That's it!" Paul must have exclaimed. God had opened the one
remaining door.[4] Across the sea was Macedonia, a region that is

---

4. God showed Paul His will through a vision. Today we have the Bible as "a lamp" and "a
light" to guide our way (Ps. 119:105). Therefore, we do not need to search our dreams or
wait for visions to confirm God's direction for us. The principles in His Word direct us to
our open doors.

part of modern-day Greece. Had Paul, in frustration, returned to Antioch earlier or stubbornly resisted the Holy Spirit's barricades in Asia, he would have missed this opportunity. Finally, the time of testing and waiting was over, and the missionaries could get to the business of evangelism.

A Person

Right away, they make preparations to cross over to Macedonia. But before leaving Troas, they add a fourth man to the team. Notice who this person is from the pronoun Luke uses in verse 10.

> And when [Paul] had seen the vision, immediately *we* sought to go into Macedonia. (v. 10a, emphasis added)

It's Luke himself![5] Possibly a citizen of Troas, Doctor Luke joins the mission as Paul's physician and as an evangelist in his own right.

Again, the closed doors in Asia are a blessing, for had it not been for them, Paul might have missed meeting Luke here in Troas.

A Call

Luke fits in well with the team. The Lord has placed the people of Macedonia on his heart too, for as the group prepares to cross the sea, he concludes "that God had called us to preach the gospel to them" (v. 10b).

In Asia, the missionaries hadn't sensed that calling, in spite of the ever-present needs around them. Christ was pointing them onward to Troas, where they could receive this call to Europe. Now they could press forward confidently, knowing Christ was with them all the way.

Message Applied

Are you searching for God's call and finding nothing but closed doors? Maybe you long to sense God's power and discover new vistas of blessing, but no matter which door you try, nothing clicks open. And you're still stumbling and groping along like Paul in a dry, barren Asia.

Whether your closed doors are sickness, failure, or frustrating circumstances, Paul's story offers two truths that will quench your parched spirit.

5. There are three "we" sections in Acts in which Luke accompanies Paul personally: 16:10–17; 20:5–21:18; and 27:1–28:16.

First, *before the Lord can turn us, He often has to stop us.* There are times when we drive through life, heading a certain direction with the cruise control on. But God has a different destination for us, so He places potholes to wake us up. Then he strews obstacles across the road so that we swerve this way and that. Finally, He sets down a solid brick wall, and we come screeching to a stop.

Now He can turn us around.

In this way, closed doors are not the end but the beginning of God's new dream for us. This fact leads us to a second truth: *when a good door closes, a better door opens.* Recall the psalmist's words:

> No good thing does He withhold from those who walk uprightly. (Ps. 84:11b)

And Jesus' words too:

> "If you then, being evil, know how to give good gifts to your children, how much more shall your Father who is in heaven give what is good to those who ask Him!" (Matt. 7:11)

God truly has our good in mind and is willing to open doors for us in His time. The issue is, Will we move through our barren Asia, trusting Him "who opens and no one will shut, and shuts and no one opens"? Or will we keep banging and pushing on closed doors?

Living Insights   STUDY ONE

Two of the most mysterious phrases in Acts are in chapter 16: "having been forbidden by the Holy Spirit to speak the word in Asia" and "the Spirit of Jesus did not permit them" (vv. 16:6b, 7b).

How did the Holy Spirit forbid them? And how were they not permitted by the Spirit of Jesus? John Stott has some suggestions:

> It may have been through giving the missionaries a strong, united inward impression, or through some outward circumstance like illness, Jewish opposition or a legal ban, or through the utterance of a Christian prophet, perhaps Silas himself (15:32).[6]

6. John Stott, *The Spirit, the Church, and the World: The Message of Acts* (Downers Grove, Ill.: InterVarsity Press, 1990), p. 260.

God may use all kinds of ways to close doors. Take some time to look at your life at present. Do you sense that God is closing a door? What causes you to believe that? (If all doors seem open now, think of a past example.)

_____

_____

What has been your response to these signs of a closed door? Have you felt frustrated? Fearful? Resistant? Are you able to accept a closed door and move on?

_____

_____

_____

How do you think you can increase your sensitivity, acceptance, and willingness when God begins to show you He's closed a door in your life?

_____

_____

_____

 ## *Living Insights*   STUDY TWO

Paul was seeking Asia when God opened up Europe. We may be seeking a certain school or career, relationship or ministry—only to have God open a door to a future far better than we imagined. This delightful, unexpected turn of events is called a serendipity.

Webster defines the word simply as "the faculty of finding valuable or agreeable things not sought for."[7] Interestingly, *serendipity* was coined by Horace Walpole, an eighteenth-century British writer who happened upon the concept in a Persian fairy tale. Lloyd John Ogilvie recounts the story.

---

7. *Webster's Ninth New Collegiate Dictionary,* see "serendipity."

The tale was about three princes of Ceylon, who had set out in search of great treasures. Though they did not find the treasure for which they searched, they were constantly surprised by more magnificent treasures they had not anticipated. . . . They grew in the realization that the true secret of an adventuresome life is in our awareness of unexpected happenings in usual circumstances.

The ancient name of the island of Ceylon is Serendip, which accounts for the title of the fascinating, impelling story of unanticipated discoveries—"The Three Princes of Serendip." From this Walpole coined the word *serendipity*.[8]

"A serendipitous life," Ogilvie explains,

is expressed in spontaneity. It is the capacity of grasping the unexpected, the freedom to respond to the unplanned.[9]

Sometimes we are afraid of open doors, even if treasure is on the other side. We may feel safer following our own predictable map. If God unexpectedly opened a door in your life, would you be spontaneous enough to enter right away, or would you hesitate?

Could God be offering you a serendipity right now? Could He be opening a door you hadn't planned on? How can you alter your course to enter that open door?

---

8. Lloyd John Ogilvie, *Drumbeat of Love* (Waco, Tex.: Word Books, Publisher, 1976), p. 200.
9. Ogilvie, *Drumbeat of Love*, p. 201

Chapter 17

A FOOTHOLD IN EUROPE
Acts 16:11–40

Remember the heartfelt wishes of that old Irish blessing?

> May the road rise up to meet you
> May the wind be always at your back.
> May the sun shine warm upon your face;
> The rains fall soft upon your fields
> And, until we meet again,
> May God hold you in the palm of His hand.[1]

If life were only like this! More often than not, the wind blasts us right in the face, knocking us back and sending us scurrying for cover. That's how Paul and his fellow missionaries must have felt when they tried in vain to bring the gospel to Asia. Gust after gust closed door after door, finally blowing them to the Aegean coast— where suddenly the winds changed. Luke records in his log:

> Putting out to sea from Troas, we ran a straight course to Samothrace, and on the day following to Neapolis. (Acts 16:11)

The phrase "ran a straight course," according to A. T. Robertson, "is a nautical term for sailing before the wind."[2] The wind was at their backs . . . obstacles and friction were gone. How free and confident they must have been as they felt the warm, favorable breezes propelling them on!

But winds are fickle; you can never quite tell when your balmy west wind will shift to a chill blast from the north, as Paul and company will again find out. God's presence and His promise, how-ever, will never leave them—no matter which way the wind blows.

---

1. "A Gaelic Blessing," as quoted in *Irish Blessings* (New York, N.Y.: Greenwich House, 1983), p. 16.

2. Archibald Thomas Robertson, *Word Pictures in the New Testament* (Grand Rapids, Mich.: Baker Book House, 1930), vol. 3, p. 249. They make the voyage in only two days—which is remarkable, considering that a later return trip will take five days to cover the same miles (see Acts 20:6).

Initial Impact: Evangelism

Sails swelling in the currents, their ship speeds without tacking to Neapolis, where they first step onto European soil. From there, Luke tells us, they walk ten miles "to Philippi, which is a leading city of the district of Macedonia, a Roman colony; and we were staying in this city for some days" (v. 12).

Paul Travels to Macedonia[3]

Philippi, a loyal Roman colony, was probably well-known to the missionaries. The townspeople had earned their citizenship by helping Caesar Augustus defeat his enemies in 42 B.C. Later, Augustus gave them a great privilege by exempting them forever from taxes.

Also, since it was situated on a sizeable hill, Philippi was a natural military outpost. Soldiers were a common sight, as were many of the trappings of Roman culture. Not as lusty as Corinth nor as sophisticated as Athens, Philippi was a more simple, straightforward city—yet still marked by immorality and paganism.

Into this city walked four Christians—the first followers of Jesus Christ anyone in this part of the world had seen. How should Paul and his partners share the gospel here? Few Jews lived in Philippi—not even enough to merit a synagogue. Where would they begin?

> On the Sabbath day we went outside the gate to a riverside, where we were supposing that there would be a place of prayer;[4] and we sat down and began speaking to the women who had assembled. (v. 13)

---

3. *Life Application® Bible*, New International Version (copublishers; Wheaton, Ill.: Tyndale House Publishers, 1991 and Grand Rapids, Mich.: Zondervan Publishing House, 1991), p. 1992. Maps © 1986, 1988 by Tyndale House Publishers, Inc. All rights reserved. Used by permission.

4. "Jewish law prescribes that wherever ten men who are heads of households reside, there a meeting place (synagogue) . . . should be built; otherwise the study of the Law in public session and corporate worship should take place in some clean area, a riverside being eminently appropriate." Richard Longenecker, *The Ministry and Message of Paul* (Grand Rapids, Mich.: Zondervan Publishing House, 1971), p. 63.

Interestingly, back at Troas Paul had seen a Macedonian man calling for help, but the first European to believe the gospel would be a Thyatiran woman.[5]

> And a certain woman named Lydia, from the city of Thyatira, a seller of purple fabrics, a worshiper of God, was listening; and the Lord opened her heart to respond to the things spoken by Paul. And when she and her household had been baptized, she urged us, saying, "If you have judged me to be faithful to the Lord, come into my house and stay." And she prevailed upon us. (vv. 14–15)

God selected Lydia, and like a flower her heart and the hearts of her family opened to Jesus. And because of her hospitality, the missionaries now had a base of operations. Their first efforts had met with success, and the wind was at their backs.

From this part of the story, we can observe a principle from Paul's actions so far: *beginning a ministry requires wisdom*. Paul could have set his mind on finding that man from Macedonia, refusing to speak to women. Instead, he wisely altered his methods to match the situation. Such flexibility, combined with sensitivity to the Spirit, are hallmarks of wise leadership. Christ's message never changes, but our methods must always mold to whatever opportunity we face.

Oppressing Opposition: Demonism

Enthusiastic about their early success, the missionaries continue to meet with and teach their new little flock. Then, along the course of their normal routine, something happened. Notice how Luke begins the next episode in the account, subtly telling us that the winds are beginning to shift.

Expression

> And it happened that as we were going to the place of prayer, a certain slave-girl having a spirit of divination met us, who was bringing her masters much

---

5. "Thyatira had been famed for centuries for its dyes. . . . Lydia herself specialized in cloth treated with an expensive purple dye, and was presumably the Macedonian agent of a Thyatiran manufacturer." John Stott, *The Spirit, the Church, and the World: The Message of Acts* (Downers Grove, Ill.: InterVarsity Press, 1990), p. 263.

profit by fortunetelling. Following after Paul and us, she kept crying out, saying, "These men are bond-servants of the Most High God, who are proclaiming to you the way of salvation." And she continued doing this for many days. (vv. 16–18a)

Apparently, a demon was speaking through this young slave woman, giving her the ability to forecast the future. Merrill Unger gives us some further insight:

> Paul's encounter with the mediumistic fortune-teller at Philippi demonstrates that not everything in fortune-telling is fraud and humbug. Real fortune-telling powers are demonic. The girl told the truth, receiving her knowledge from demons. . . . Her commendation of Paul and Silas as "servants of the most high God" . . . demonstrates the subtlety of Satan in gaining followers for later deception. . . . The incident shows how Satan frequently parades as an angel of light, especially under the guise of alleged religiosity.[6]

To us, her announcement seems helpful to the cause of Christ—she's telling the people where they can find out about the salvation of their souls. But it was really a clever ruse of Satan, designed to infiltrate the infant church. For the Greek actually says, "These men . . . are proclaiming to you *a* way of salvation." In other words, she was saying, "You have a way of salvation, we have a way of salvation—let's join forces!" In this way Satan could siphon Christ's group into his own. And the girl proclaimed this day after day, every day.

Exorcism

Finally, annoyed by her incessant ploy to poison the ministry, Paul

> turned and said to the spirit, "I command you in the name of Jesus Christ to come out of her!" And it came out at that very moment. (v. 18b)

---

6. Merrill F. Unger, *Demons in the World Today* (Wheaton, Ill.: Tyndale House Publishers, 1971), p. 63.

Note Paul's method in casting out this wicked spirit: (1) He was not intimidated, but in full control. (2) He spoke directly to the demon, not the girl. (3) He commanded it to come out of her; he didn't ask. (4) He drew on the power of Jesus, not his own strength. And in an instant, the demon, the voice, and the fortune-telling ability were gone.

This episode brings us to a second principle: *in every major breakthrough there is a corresponding resistance.* For every step forward, the devil will meet you halfway. And for every new strategy you implement, he will mount a corresponding counterattack. But we are never to be intimidated by his evil presence, and we are never to give in—two things easy to do if we try to oppose him in our own strength. We have Christ's power, though, and we can stand fast in Him. For, as Scripture says,

> greater is He who is in you than he who is in the world. (1 John 4:4b)

Physical Pain: Mistreatment

With the demon gone, you'd think the warm breezes would return for Paul, Silas, Timothy, and Luke. However, just up ahead looms a monstrous, churning squall.

Beaten and Imprisoned

> When her masters saw that their hope of profit was gone, they seized Paul and Silas and dragged them into the market place before the authorities, and when they had brought them to the chief magistrates, they said, "These men are throwing our city into confusion, being Jews, and are proclaiming customs which it is not lawful for us to accept or to observe, being Romans." And the crowd rose up together against them, and the chief magistrates tore their robes off them, and proceeded to order them to be beaten with rods. And when they had inflicted many blows upon them, they threw them into prison, commanding the jailer to guard them securely; and he, having received such a command, threw them into the inner prison, and fastened their feet in the stocks. (Acts 16:19–24)

Three volatile elements combined to stir up this hurricane of trouble. The first was *greed*. The girl's masters cared nothing for her well-being; they just wanted to use her. If her soul being ravaged by hell brought them a profit, that was fine with them. But threaten their precious income, and they want revenge. A second element was *prejudice*. Did you notice the subtle way they slipped in the part about the missionaries "being Jews" (v. 20b)? The third catalyst of this chaos was *exaggeration and lies*. Paul and his men weren't "throwing the city into confusion"; neither were they proclaiming unlawful customs. They'd only done what was right.

Such slander, however, convinced the townspeople that the missionaries were dangerous infiltrators deserving punishment. With no attempt to hear the facts or hold court, the mob attacked them and threw them into prison. Any cries for mercy by Paul and Silas were drowned out in the roaring storm of hatred.

Prayer and Praise

How would you respond under such mistreatment? You've been lied about, beaten, thrown in a dungeon, and locked in stocks. Every breath painfully reminds you of your cracked ribs and bruised kidneys. Your back aches; your leg muscles cramp. Rats scurry across the floor in the dark. Feel like singing?

> About midnight Paul and Silas were praying and singing hymns of praise to God, and the prisoners were listening to them. (v. 25)

In the midst of their pain, they're praising God! And down the hall, other inmates are listening, amazed as we are that they could be joyful in such a miserable situation. Even in prison, the gospel is shining.

Deliverance and Salvation

"Suddenly there came a great earthquake" (v. 26a). In His perfect timing, God steps out of the cell's shadows and makes His presence felt by everyone.

> The foundations of the prison house were shaken; and immediately all the doors were opened, and everyone's chains were unfastened. (v. 26b)

Imagine the jailer's panic—all these inmates whom he had cruelly bound in torturous stocks were now freed! And if they didn't kill him in revenge, his captain would do the job as punishment for letting them escape. So he decided to beat them to it. But just as he was about to plunge his sword into himself,

> Paul cried out with a loud voice, saying, "Do yourself no harm, for we are all here!" And he called for lights and rushed in and, trembling with fear, he fell down before Paul and Silas, and after he brought them out, he said, "Sirs, what must I do to be saved?" And they said, "Believe in the Lord Jesus, and you shall be saved, you and your household." And they spoke the word of the Lord to him together with all who were in his house. And he took them that very hour of the night and washed their wounds, and immediately he was baptized, he and all his household. And he brought them into his house and set food before them, and rejoiced greatly, having believed in God with his whole household. (vv. 27–34)

By caring for the jailer's welfare, Paul and Silas revealed the mercy of Christ to him. And this taste of Jesus' compassion made the jailer long for more. When he trusted Christ, forgiveness washed over his soul and changed his life forever. He who inflicted the wounds now bathed the wounds of Paul and Silas in his own home. They in turn washed him in baptism—a moving scene of God's grace.

This part of the story illustrates a third principle: *praise in hard times reaps a harvest of benefits.* Paul and Silas could have given in to despair and doubt, but they chose to believe that God's unseen hand was still there working things out for their good. And from this wellspring of trust, praise bubbled forth, ministering to their fellow prisoners and probably their own hearts as well. But the greatest result their attitude brought was the eternal life of a man and his whole family. A harvest that makes all the pain in sowing worthwhile.

Remarkable Release: Encouragement

Still bursting with joy, the newfound friends return to the prison so as not to arouse the suspicion of the jailer's superiors. They'll be hearing from those superiors soon enough—with a surprising message.

Now when day came, the chief magistrates sent their policemen, saying, "Release those men." And the jailer reported these words to Paul, saying, "The chief magistrates have sent to release you. Now therefore, come out and go in peace." But Paul said to them, "They have beaten us in public without trial, men who are Romans, and have thrown us into prison; and now are they sending us away secretly? No indeed! But let them come themselves and bring us out."[7] (vv. 35–37)

Rather than accept the officials' perfunctory release, Paul pulls an ace out of his sleeve; for besides being exempt from taxes, Roman citizens had other privileges, such as "freedom from scourging, from arrest except in extreme cases, and the right to appeal to the emperor."[8] What an embarrassment for a colony proud of its Roman ties to treat Roman citizens like this! When the policemen conveyed Paul's message, the alarmed officials

came and appealed to them, and when they had brought them out, they kept begging them to leave the city. And they went out of the prison and entered the house of Lydia, and when they saw the brethren, they encouraged them and departed. (vv. 39–40)

God was bringing light out of a dark situation, which demonstrates a final principle: *God's victories are always overwhelming.* If we let Him fight our battles, we are assured we will conquer through Christ (Rom. 8:35–37). We must be sensitive, though, to His moving, for His ways are often different than we expect.

For Paul, Silas, Timothy, and Luke, the wind was shifting back again as they traveled on to the next city. Philippi had taught them a lesson they would never forget—a lesson we would do well to learn. With a few changes, the old Irish blessing sums it up best:

---

7. "Likely, Paul had anticipated the course of events . . . and determined to withhold the information [that they were Roman citizens] until it would count for the most on behalf of the group of disciples he was leaving behind in Philippi. When the Roman officials realized their mistake, they would be inclined to avoid taking any illegal steps against members of the infant church." Everett F. Harrison, *Interpreting Acts: The Expanding Church* (Grand Rapids, Mich.: Zondervan Publishing House, Academie Books, 1986), p. 274.

8. R. C. H. Lenski, *The Interpretation of the Acts of the Apostles* (Columbus, Ohio: Wartburg Press, 1944), p. 652.

Even if the road crumbles before you,
Or the wind is at your face;
If the sun beats hot upon you,
Or the storms destroy your fields;
Even if we never meet again,
Remember, God will still hold you in the palm of
His hand.

 Living Insights

When we read the story of the demon-possessed slave girl and her mercenary masters, we are outraged at their callous exploitation of her—and rightly so. For using another human being is one of the deepest kinds of immorality. Author Neil Gallagher writes:

> In our universe, there is a wide, thick, eternal line. Above the line are people, below the line are things.
> People are to be loved. Things are to be used.
> Immorality is the reversal. It's immoral to love things. It's immoral to use people.
> It's immoral to use people for *any* reason. It's immoral to use people for political, racial, financial, or sexual advantage. People who are used are people who hate.
> . . . Immorality ravages people.[9]

We who bear Christ's name have not been called to ravage one another, to dehumanize those who are made in Christ's very image. Instead, we are to love one another just as He has loved us (John 15:12); work for each other's best interests (Phil. 2:3–5); and build up each other's lives so we can reach the fullness of Christ (Eph. 4:15–16).

In the days that follow, meditate on Christ's words, on Gallagher's words, on the awesome power and profound working of love. And as you relate to others—Christians and non-Christians alike—ponder the motives in your heart. Make sure love of people is your driving force, not love of what they can do for you.

9. Neil Gallagher, *How to Stop the Porno Plague* (Minneapolis, Minn.: Bethany Fellowship, 1977), pp. 45–46.

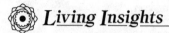 *Living Insights*

How could Paul and Silas sing in prison? Most of us would be plotting our revenge, calling our lawyers, nursing our sore bodies, and consoling our bruised egos.

How would you respond to such severe mistreatment?

_____

_____

In Paul's letter to Lydia, the jailer, and the other Philippian believers, he helps us understand how he could sing in prison. According to Philippians 1:29–30, what was happening to the Christians in Philippi at this time?

_____

According to verse 27a, what is his singular command to them?

_____

If they follow his advice, what will be the results (vv. 27b–28)?

_____

_____

When we conduct ourselves "in a manner worthy of the gospel of Christ," we behave in a way that attracts others to Him. Remember how Paul's attitude attracted the jailer to Jesus? If you're being mistreated now, how can you act so that others will see the beauty of Christ?

_____

_____

_____

_____

Chapter 18

NECK DEEP IN GREECE

Acts 17:1–15

I t is possible to be living, yet not fully alive.

We can be like those who look and act like they're "doing it right" but are really an empty show—not really connecting with other people, not seeing the meaning in their everyday lives. Or we can be the kind of person John Powell describes in his book *Fully Human, Fully Alive:*

> Fully alive human beings are alive in their external and internal *senses*. . . . They smell the fragrance of each new day and taste the deliciousness of every moment. . . .
>
> Fully alive people are also alive in their *minds*. They are very much aware of the wisdom in the statement of Socrates that "the unreflected life isn't worth living." . . . Most of all, perhaps, these people are alive in *will* and *heart*. They love much.[1]

Powell admits, though, that fully alive people are not necessarily happy all the time. "The fullness of life," he writes,

> must not be misrepresented as the proverbial "bowl of cherries." Fully alive people, precisely because they are fully alive, obviously experience failure as well as success. They are open to both pain and pleasure. They have many questions and some answers. They cry and they laugh. They dream and they hope. The only things that remain alien to their experience of life are passivity and apathy. They say a strong "yes" to life and a resounding "amen" to love. They feel the strong stings of growing—of going from the old into the new—but their sleeves are always rolled up, their minds are whirring, and their hearts are ablaze.[2]

1. John Powell, *Fully Human, Fully Alive* (Allen, Tex.: Tabor Publishing, 1976), pp. 20–21.

2. Powell, *Fully Human, Fully Alive*, pp. 21–22.

Enthusiasm. Zeal. Drive. Vision. These are the characteristics of a person who is fully alive—a person just like the apostle Paul. Studying his journeys is like taking a field trip on the subject of full living. So let's lace up our hiking boots and try to keep up with him on the next leg of his travels—the part of his journey in Europe where we find him and his companions, shall we say, neck deep in Greece!

Transition: Philippi to Thessalonica

The road from Philippi to Thessalonica was rocky at first. Paul and Silas had been beaten and imprisoned, then escorted out of town by the embarrassed and apologetic officials. But before leaving Philippi, the missionaries took time to encourage the new believers. Most likely, they also decided that Luke should stay behind to further help the Philippian Christians. We assume this because the "we" references in the account suddenly change to "they," as if Luke were saying, "They went on, but I didn't go with them."

So Paul, Silas, and Timothy waved good-bye to Luke and the new believers, and

> when they had traveled through Amphipolis and Apollonia, they came to Thessalonica. (Acts 17:1a)

Ministry in Thessalonica

Following the Egnatian Way, the main highway through Macedonia, the three missionaries arrived in Thessalonica ready for action.

City and Government

The travelers' first sight of the city must have taken their breath away, for Thessalonica was the crown jewel of

Ministry in Macedonia[3]

Macedonia, placed in a striking setting on the Thermaic Gulf by the Aegean Sea. Behind it rose the majestic mountains of Greece,

3. *Life Application® Bible*, New International Version (copublishers; Wheaton, Ill.: Tyndale House Publishers, 1991 and Grand Rapids, Mich.: Zondervan Publishing House, 1991), p. 1994. Maps © 1986, 1988 by Tyndale House Publishers, Inc. All rights reserved. Used by permission.

including the fabled Mount Olympus. It also lay right in the path of one of the major thoroughfares of the day and had a fine harbor, making it a chief center of commerce and military strength. And nearby hot springs lent the city the ambience of a fashionable luxury resort. Thessalonica also had special privileges no other city in the region had. Everett Harrison explains:

> In contrast to Philippi, which was a Roman colony, Thessalonica was a free city; that is, it was not subject to the provincial administration in local affairs and could pass its own laws and have its own institutions. . . . In addition to its rulers, who were called "politarchs," it had its own popular assembly.[4]

This is the free-spirited, influential backdrop for Paul's newest adventure. Here, as at Philippi, he will demonstrate his enthusiasm for life as he attempts to bring the light of Christ to this sparkling but spiritually dark city.

Method and Message

Paul's enthusiasm appears soon after he arrives in Thessalonica, where he heads directly to

> a synagogue of the Jews. And according to Paul's custom, he went to them, and for three Sabbaths reasoned with them from the Scriptures, explaining and giving evidence that the Christ had to suffer and rise again from the dead, and saying, "This Jesus whom I am proclaiming to you is the Christ." (vv. 1b–3)

Tirelessly, Paul taught the truths of Christ to the people. He didn't force the message on them. Rather, he was patient, showing respect for the people and allowing them to choose for themselves. In this manner, he communicated the gospel using an effective three-pronged approach.

First, he "reasoned with them." *Reasoned* in Greek means "to select, distinguish, then to revolve in the mind."[5] Carefully dipping into the only Scriptures available to him, the Old Testament, Paul

---

4. Everett F. Harrison, *Interpreting Acts: The Expanding Church* (Grand Rapids, Mich.: Zondervan Publishing House, Academie Books, 1986), p. 275.

5. Archibald Thomas Robertson, *Word Pictures in the New Testament* (Grand Rapids, Mich.: Baker Book House, 1930), vol. 3, p. 267.

brought up key messianic passages as food for thought. Second, he *explained* or opened these passages, making them clear so the people could see that the Messiah must die and rise again. Third, he gave *evidence*. The nuance of this word communicates the idea that he placed his own illustrations alongside Scripture to strengthen his argument. Then he made his conclusion: "This Jesus whom I am proclaiming to you is the Christ."

Paul presented the gospel accurately, clearly, and practically; but according to his epistle, he did so "amid much opposition" (1 Thess. 2:2b).[6] Despite the struggle, he remained zealous for Christ and His message, alive to both his purpose and his pressures.

Response and Escape

Like magnets, some people are drawn closer to Paul's teaching and others are repelled by it. According to Acts 17:4, three groups are attracted to the gospel:

> And some of them were persuaded and joined Paul and Silas, along with a great multitude of the God-fearing Greeks and a number of the leading women.

Although "a great multitude" of Gentiles and "a number of the leading women" respond, only "some" of the Jews are persuaded to follow Christ. This illustrates the fact that what influences one person may not convince the next. When we seek to persuade people with the gospel, we must leave them room to respond according to their hearts' leading.

Also, it is interesting that the large number of Greeks "turned to God from idols" (see 1 Thess. 1:9), yet Paul had not mentioned idols in his synagogue talks—only Christ. Paul's example teaches us to focus our witnessing on Christ, not peripherals, and to persuade but not manipulate nonbelievers to trust Him. What balance Paul exhibited! He firmly presented solid facts about Christ, yet he still gave people the dignity and freedom to think, consider, and wrestle with their decisions. They could accept or reject the gospel, and unfortunately, many chose the latter.

---

6. The Greek word for *opposition* is *agōn*. We derive our word *agony* from this word, and here it "implies the intense effort and strenuous exertion in Paul's preaching the gospel especially in the [face] of hostility and conflict which he had with the Jews." Fritz Rienecker, *A Linguistic Key to the Greek New Testament* (Grand Rapids, Mich.: Zondervan Publishing House, Regency Reference Library, 1980), p. 589.

> But the Jews, becoming jealous and taking along
> some wicked men from the market place, formed a
> mob and set the city in an uproar; and coming upon
> the house of Jason, they were seeking to bring them
> out to the people. (Acts 17:5)

Clothed in the same garb of jealousy that enwrapped Jesus' antagonists, the Jewish leaders stirred up an angry lynch mob with the help of some of the city's hoodlums and loafers—men they would otherwise disdain. Shouting and shaking their fists, the frenzied citizens swarmed around Jason's house, where the missionaries had been staying. Unable to find Paul and his companions, they expend their violent rage by

> dragging Jason and some brethren before the city
> authorities, shouting, "These men who have upset
> the world have come here also; and Jason has wel-
> comed them, and they all act contrary to the decrees
> of Caesar, saying that there is another king, Jesus."
> And they stirred up the crowd and the city authori-
> ties who heard these things. (vv. 6b–8)

Easily manipulated by public opinion, the city authorities, or "politarchs," accept the false accusations. Employing the same tactic the Pharisees used against Jesus (see Luke 23:1–2), the Jewish leaders accused the missionaries of high treason. They even said these three unlikely desperadoes had "upset the world"—an exaggeration that actually rings with an element of truth. Christianity was upsetting the world, not by turning people upside down, but by turning them right side up.

With no day in court, the missionaries are pronounced guilty. Apparently, Jason's only way to protect their lives as well as the future of the Thessalonian church is to sign an agreement guaranteeing that the missionaries would leave and never return.[7] This satisfies the crowd, so that

> when they had received a pledge from Jason and the
> others, they released them.

---

7. "It was probably this legal ban which Paul saw as Satan preventing him from returning to Thessalonica" (see 1 Thess. 2:18). John Stott, *The Spirit, the Church, and the World: The Message of Acts* (Downers Grove, Ill.: InterVarsity Press, 1990), p. 273.

> And the brethren immediately sent Paul and
> Silas away by night to Berea. (Acts 17:9–10a)

Ministry in Berea

The missionaries must have left Thessalonica frustrated. Yet indomitable Paul would not quit; he targets another town for the gospel, and away they go.

Off the main highway, Berea is a smaller community located about fifty miles from Thessalonica. The atmosphere is different here: "these [Jews] were more noble-minded than those in Thessalonica" (v. 11a). The air isn't filled with prejudice or jealousy; rather, the people are sensitive and responsive to the truth. As a result, their approach to Scripture and Paul's teaching is refreshingly complementary.

> They received the word with great eagerness, examining the Scriptures daily, to see whether these things were so. Many of them therefore believed, along with a number of prominent Greek women and men. (vv. 11b–12)

Throughout church history, the Bereans have been models of how to discern truthful teaching—they examined the Bible closely, checking everything Paul was telling them. How dangerous it is for us to blindly accept what people teach without studying the Scriptures for ourselves! That is how cults get started. Examining the Scriptures daily like the Bereans did shows us whose teaching to follow.

For the missionaries, these must have been satisfying days. Only "some" Jews had believed in Thessalonica, but "many" Jews believed in Berea. The whole town seemed to be responding to the gospel, until . . .

> When the Jews of Thessalonica found out that the word of God had been proclaimed by Paul in Berea also, they came there likewise, agitating and stirring up the crowds. And then immediately the brethren sent Paul out to go as far as the sea; and Silas and Timothy remained there. Now those who conducted Paul brought him as far as Athens; and receiving a command for Silas and Timothy to come to him as soon as possible, they departed. (vv. 13–15)

With Luke left behind in Philippi and Silas and Timothy in Berea, Paul found himself in the big city of Athens all alone. But he could look back on his experiences in Macedonia and reassure himself that the believers there were in God's hands. He was not the focus of their lives—he had been forced out of the picture before that could happen. God was the center of their worship, and that's exactly the way Paul wanted it.

Application: Then and Now

If Paul's life teaches us anything, it's that fully alive people don't always have it easy. They do, however, know how to handle life's storms with enthusiasm, grace, and balance. If you desire to live life to the fullest like Paul, here's a little prestorm advice based on Paul's journey.

First, *remember that determination is at the heart of any accomplishment.* Paul had the courage to stay on his course in spite of imprisonments, beatings, and public slander. If we have that same determination, we, too, can accomplish great things for God.

Second, be forewarned that *rejection is to be expected when truth is declared.* In fact, if nobody rejects it, we probably aren't telling the whole truth! People easily believe Satan's lies; it's God's pure Word they have trouble swallowing. So expect rejection, but remember they are really rejecting God, not you.

Third, unfortunately, *appreciation is seldom expressed at the right time.* Paul never once had an autograph-signing party. There were no banquets in his honor or paid vacation trips just to say thanks. Fully alive people can survive without those kudos. But they can't survive without encouragement, and our most unfailing source of that is Christ. He's the one cheering us on, reminding us what we're fighting for, and supplying us the power to win the victory.

After all, it's His life in us that truly makes us fully alive.

 Living Insights STUDY ONE

A child in pajamas bounding down the stairs on Christmas morning, a ponytailed cheerleader bouncing to the rhythm of a victory chant—these are the images that come to mind when we think of enthusiasm.

But the word means more than just unabashed joy. It is derived from the Greek word *enthousiasmos*, which means "inspiration" and is based on two Greek words: *en* and *theos*[8]—"in" and "God." In a sense, to be enthusiastic is to be inspired by God.

To be fully alive, as Paul was, we must have this kind of enthusiasm—this divine fire. Are you fanning these flames, or are you busy dousing them with fear, pessimism, doubt, or something else? Take a look at the following areas to see if any need to be rekindled.

- How do you respond to change?_____

_____

- How do you respond to progress?_____

_____

- How do you respond when bad things happen?_____

_____

If your enthusiasm for life is flickering in one of these areas, how can you stoke the divine fire in your heart? Take some time to think through a workable strategy.

_____

_____

_____

 Living Insights STUDY TWO

Would you be able to show that Jesus is the Christ by using only the Old Testament? If you ever try to share your faith with a Jew, the ability to do so would be indispensable. Take a moment to look up the following messianic passages. As you read through them, use your Bible's margin notes or a concordance to find the corresponding New Testament passages. Jot them down as you go along.

_____

8. *Webster's Ninth New Collegiate Dictionary*, see "enthusiasm."

Psalm 16:10–11 _____

Psalm 22:1, 11–18 _____

Psalm 110:1 _____

Isaiah 7:14 _____

Isaiah 9:6–7 _____

Isaiah 52:13–53:12 _____

Now try your hand at "reasoning," "explaining and giving evidence." Write out what you would say to a Jewish friend.

_____

_____

_____

_____

_____

_____

And remember to follow Paul's example when you do share: be patient and respect your friend's right to choose.

Chapter 19

AREOPAGUS EGGHEADS VERSUS A SEED-PICKER

Acts 17:16–34

How old was Jack Dempsey when he won the heavyweight crown? When did Paderewski write his *Minuet in G*? What is the name of the Aztec god of the dead? Tough questions. But not for the Quiz Kids.

For those under grandparent age who've never heard of the Quiz Kids, it was a radio show back in the days of "Fibber McGee and Molly" and "The Shadow." It pitted pint-sized Einsteins against one another, answering questions that would stump most adults. Fighting for the buzzer, these junior geniuses would smugly announce the answer, tossing in a few obscure details to show off. There was nothing more intimidating for youngsters of that era than to be compared by their parents to a Quiz Kid!

One wonders, though, what ever happened to these prodigies when they grew up. Some probably became engineers or scientists or professors at MIT or Harvard. Still brilliant, still intimidating. But no matter what they've accomplished or how bright they are, one fact remains: they have the same spiritual need the rest of us do—Christ.

At the Areopagus in Athens, Paul faced a group of highbrow, grown-up quiz kids. Was he intimidated? Maybe. But nothing could stop Paul when it came to talking about Christ.

Athens: A City of Extremes

Athens had been home to Socrates, Plato, Aristotle—the greatest ancient philosophers. The entire city, in fact, was a showcase of past intellectual achievement.[1] But the people of Athens still hungered for spiritual things. That hunger was most evident in what

---

1. For centuries, Athens had been the cradle of democracy and education. Rome respected the city for its highly developed culture so much that "in consideration of her splendid past, the Romans left Athens free to carry on her own institutions as a free and allied city within the Roman Empire." F. F. Bruce, *Commentary on the Book of Acts*, The New International Commentary on the New Testament series, ed. F. F. Bruce (Grand Rapids, Mich.: William B. Eerdmans Publishing Co., 1954), p. 348.

Paul first noticed about the city—something that disturbed his soul. While waiting for Luke to join him from Philippi and Silas and Timothy from Berea, Paul's "spirit was being provoked within him as he was beholding the city full of idols" (Acts 17:16).

Tens of thousands of idols had been cut into the public buildings, stationed along the streets, and memorialized in shrines and temples. According to R. C. H. Lenski, even the ancient historians were amazed by the vast number of them.

> Petronius satirically remarks that in Athens it was easier to find a god than a man. In his fine description Pausanias states that Athens had more images than all Greece put together. Xenophon calls Athens "one great altar, one great offering to the gods."[2]

Paul: A Man of Courage

Determined to plant God's flag of truth in this dark, idolatrous city, Paul first scopes out more familiar territory.

In the Synagogue

As is his habit, he begins evangelizing the city by "reasoning in the synagogue with the Jews and the God-fearing Gentiles" (v. 17a), selecting familiar passages from the Old Testament to prove that Jesus is the Messiah. But his heart breaks for the idolatrous pagans outside the synagogue walls. So he takes his message to the streets.

At the Marketplace

The marketplace provides the perfect platform. Here the Athenians mix and mingle, idly shopping for the newest fashions and the latest philosophies. So here Paul goes, speaking "every day with those who happened to be present" (v. 17b). In no time, two groups of thinkers start reacting to this curious foreigner and his new teaching.

> Some of the Epicurean and Stoic philosophers were conversing with him. And some were saying, "What would this idle babbler wish to say?" Others, "He seems to be a proclaimer of strange deities,"—because he was preaching Jesus and the resurrection. (v. 18)

2. R. C. H. Lenski, *The Interpretation of the Acts of the Apostles* (Columbus, Ohio: Wartburg Press, 1944), p. 708.

Who were the Epicureans and the Stoics? Philosophers at widely divergent ends of the spectrum. Epicureans believed in a universe of chance and remote gods, of any pleasure that would not bring pain, of death as the ultimate finality.[3] Stoics, on the other hand, were pantheists who saw God within every material thing; they were fatalistic and unemotional, considering apathy their highest virtue.[4]

Imagine them in their philosophers' robes, stroking their beards as they circle Paul and size him up, kicking the tires of his new teaching. Some of them shake their heads and call him a "babbler"—a *spermologos* in Greek. F. F. Bruce explains that the word literally means "seed-picker," like a gutter sparrow, and was used here to describe "one who picked up scraps of learning here and there and purveyed them where he could."[5] Others, though, are curious about Paul's teaching—especially about Jesus and the resurrection. They know of Zeus, but who is Jesus?

As they consult with one another, they come to a decision: Take him to the Areopagus!

On the Areopagus

The Areopagus, sometimes called Mars Hill after the Roman god of war, Mars, had

> an important tribunal in Athens, including among
> its many responsibilities the supervision of education
> in the city and the controlling of the many itinerant
> lecturers passing through.[6]

Weaving their way through the marketplace with Paul in tow, the philosophers finally arrive before the Areopagites and wait for their curiosity to be sated.

> "May we know what this new teaching is which you
> are proclaiming? For you are bringing some strange

---

3. See William Barclay, *The Acts of the Apostles*, rev. ed., The Daily Study Bible Series (Philadelphia, Pa.: Westminster Press, 1976), p. 130.

4. See Ray Stedman, *Acts 13–20: Growth of the Body* (Santa Ana, Calif.: Vision House Publishers, 1976), pp. 116–17.

5. Bruce, *Acts*, p. 351.

6. See Richard Longenecker, *The Ministry and Message of Paul* (Grand Rapids, Mich.: Zondervan Publishing House, 1971), p. 65.

things to our ears; we want to know therefore what these things mean." (Now all the Athenians and the strangers visiting there used to spend their time in nothing other than telling or hearing something new.) (vv. 19b–21)

Paul surveys the men on this elite council, the highest court in Athens. A cultural richness and hushed awe fills the air. It was a majestic yet intimidating place. But the "seed-picker" of Tarsus knows exactly what to do. He speaks eloquently and clearly, not about philosophy or culture, but about God and His Son.

Address: A Message of Impact

With no time to prepare, Paul fashions a brief address, but one in which every word counts. Five factors stand out that we would do well to heed as we communicate our faith with others.

He Started Where They Were

Standing before the prestigious council, Paul begins,

"Men of Athens, I observe that you are very religious in all respects. For while I was passing through and examining the objects of your worship, I also found an altar with this inscription, 'TO AN UNKNOWN GOD.'" (vv. 22b–23a)

He didn't start with the Creation, Old Testament Scripture, Christ, or sin—concepts that were foreign to his audience. Instead, he opened with a subject close to home: religion. He wasn't attempting to flatter them, either; he was just stating as fact that a city displaying so many idols must contain people interested in religion.

He Used the Familiar to Introduce the Unfamiliar

Using the familiar—the subject of religion and their altar to an unknown god—he had turned their attention in a smooth transition to the unfamiliar: the subject of the living God whom they did not know.

"What therefore you worship in ignorance, this I proclaim to you. The God who made the world and all things in it." (vv. 23b–24a)

To them, God was unknown; but Paul's point was that He was not unknowable. With all the care of an architectural engineer, Paul was methodically constructing a bridge that would hopefully span the gap between their ignorance and the truth of Christ.

He Developed His Theme Forcefully and Clearly

Speaking in terms they could relate to and understand, Paul continues,

> "Since He is Lord of heaven and earth, [God] does not dwell in temples made with hands; neither is He served by human hands, as though He needed anything, since He Himself gives to all life and breath and all things; and He made from one, every nation of mankind to live on all the face of the earth, having determined their appointed times, and the boundaries of their habitation, that they should seek God, if perhaps they might grope for Him and find Him, though He is not far from each one of us; for in Him we live and move and exist." (vv. 24b–28a)

Pulling back the veil of heaven, Paul reveals four key facts about God. First, being the Creator, God cannot be contained (v. 24)—which told the Athenians that their temples and shrines wouldn't do. Second, being the originator, He has no needs (v. 25). They could not give Him anything He didn't have or tell Him anything He didn't know; He is self-sufficient. Third, being intelligent, He has a definite plan (vv. 26–27). He is in control, yet unlike the Epicureans' or Stoics' gods, He is accessible and approachable. Fourth, being the sustainer, He is not dependent (v. 28a). Rather, we are dependent on Him—His grace, mercy, and love.

He Kept Their Attention with Relevant Illustrations

Many of us are familiar with these facts about God. But to the Athenians, this was a banquet of new truth. So Paul helps them digest it by using illustrations.

> "As even some of your own poets have said, 'For we also are His offspring.'" (v. 28b)

Quoting Aratus, a Greek poet, he tries to convince them that God is their Creator by showing that even their own poets believed in a creator-god. How astute Paul was in taking this poem about

Zeus and revealing that its true subject is Christ![7]

He Applied the Message, Personally

Their philosophers had always discussed comfortable ideas, but Paul brings his truths much more close to home—uncomfortably close.

> "Being then the offspring of God, we ought not to think that the Divine Nature is like gold or silver or stone, an image formed by the art and thought of man. Therefore having overlooked the times of ignorance, God is now declaring to men that all everywhere should repent, because He has fixed a day in which He will judge the world in righteousness through a Man whom He has appointed, having furnished proof to all men by raising Him from the dead." (vv. 29–31)

God was not only their creator, He was their judge. Actions today impacted their lives beyond the grave, where the resurrected Jesus awaits. But here was a stumbling block. Since childhood, the Athenians had heard a certain motto denying bodily resurrection: "Once a man dies and the earth drinks up his blood, there is *no resurrection*."[8] How would they react to this aspect of Paul's teaching?

Response: A Reaction of Conflict

Luke's conclusion of this episode reveals the Athenians' three responses:

> Now when they heard of the resurrection of the dead, some began to sneer, but others said, "We shall hear you again concerning this." So Paul went out of their midst. But some men joined him and believed, among whom also was Dionysius the Areopagite and a woman named Damaris and others with them. (vv. 32–34)

Some of them openly rejected Paul and his teaching. Some put

7. The entire poem read: "Never, O men, let us leave him unmentioned. All ways are full of Zeus and all meeting-places of men; the sea and the harbors are full of him. In every direction we all have to do with Zeus; for we are also his offspring." Bruce, *Acts*, p. 360.

8. Bruce, *Acts*, pp. 363–64.

off the decsion, saying they would get back with him later. But others believed, one of whom was Dionysius, a member of the Areopagus council.

This is the last we hear of Athens and these few believers in the book of Acts. Luke doesn't even tell us if a church was established here. Still, the story confronts us with the same decision the Athenians had to make. Is God unknown to us? Are we, too, worshiping in ignorance?

Through God's Word, we can know Him. It is true, as Paul told the intelligentsia of Athens so many centuries ago, "He is not far from each one of us" (v. 27).

 ## Living Insights

Many of us can talk comfortably with non-Christians about almost any subject . . . except Jesus Christ. If His name enters the conversation, we freeze up. Doubts like icicles suddenly start dripping down our backs. "My comments sound so trite." "I'm not even making sense!" "Does my friend comprehend anything I'm saying?" Drip . . . drip . . . drip.

The five principles of sharing Christ that Paul modeled can boost your confidence by helping you communicate more effectively. Think of a non-Christian friend or relative to whom you'd like to witness. How can you start where he or she is? What are this person's primary concerns? Family? Future? Health? List some of them.

_____

_____

How can you use these familiar subjects as a bridge to the unfamiliar subject of Christ?

_____

_____

What facts can you give about Christ that will explain the gospel more forcefully and clearly?[9]

9. The tract *Knowing God Personally* is an excellent tool to use in explaining the gospel. You can purchase it from Sonlife Ministries, Moody Bible Institute, 820 North LaSalle Drive, Chicago, Illinois 60610.

_____

_____

_____

What situations or events from his or her life can you draw upon to illustrate Christ—His love, mercy, salvation, and so on?

_____

_____

What can you say to help him or her apply the gospel personally?

_____

_____

_____

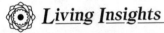 **_Living Insights_**

Paul spoke about Christ not only in the synagogue but also in the marketplace, "with those who happened to be present" (17:17b).

With your mind's eye, take a glance around your "marketplace" and see who is present. There's the person who smiles at you from behind a counter, the one who stares straight ahead in the elevator, or who sits quietly in the park. You know the names of a few of them, like the custodian or the security guard, the briefcase-carrying executive or the rope-skipping little girl. Your marketplace—that's where Paul would be. Because that's where Jesus would be.

As you read the following poem by George MacLeod, ask the Lord for His eyes to see the needy people in your world and His courage to point them to the Cross.

> I simply argue that the cross be raised again
> at the center of the market place
> as well as on the steeple of the church,
>
> I am recovering the claim that
> Jesus was not crucified in a cathedral
> between two candles:

But on a cross between two thieves;
   on a town garbage heap;
   At a crossroad of politics so cosmopolitan
   that they had to write His title
   in Hebrew and in Latin and in Greek . . .

And at the kind of place where cynics talk smut,
   and thieves curse and soldiers gamble.

Because that is where He died,
   and that is what He died about.
   And that is where Christ's men ought to be,
   and what church people ought to be about.[10]

10. George MacLeod, as quoted by Charles R. Swindoll in *Strengthening Your Grip* (Dallas, Tex.: Word Publishing, 1982), p. 26. Taken from *Focal Point*, the Conservative Baptist Theological Seminary Bulletin, Spring, 1981.

Chapter 20

A CORINTHIAN-
CALIFORNIAN IMPACT
Acts 18:1–18a

> After these things [Paul] left Athens and went to
> Corinth. (Acts 18:1)

A seemingly simple, straightforward sentence, isn't it? Paul left one city and went to another. Nothing complicated about that. At least, not on the surface.

Underneath, however, are the foreboding rumblings and crackings of an earthquake and its jolting aftershock. Athens' myriad idols and stagnant arrogance had been the first temblor to rattle the devoutly monotheistic Apostle. But it will be Corinth's debauchery, like the overwhelming shock of a second jolt, that will threaten to knock Paul off his feet.

Obvious Facts about Corinth

When Paul arrived in Corinth, it was as if he stepped off a bus in one of California's seedier districts—like San Francisco's Tenderloin or Hollywood's Sunset Strip. And like its California cousins, Corinth was no shantytown, but a city of voluptuous wealth. John Stott provides a little background information for us.

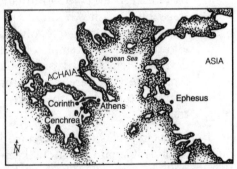

Ministry in Corinth and Ephesus[1]

Situated close to the isthmus which joined mainland

---

1. *Life Application® Bible*, New International Version (copublishers; Wheaton, Ill.: Tyndale House Publishers, 1991 and Grand Rapids, Mich.: Zondervan Publishing House, 1991), p. 1997. Maps © 1986, 1988 by Tyndale House Publishers, Inc. All rights reserved. Used by permission.

Greece to the Peloponnesian peninsula, it commanded the trade routes in all directions, not only north-south by land but also east-west by sea. For before the Corinthian canal was cut for three and a half miles across the isthmus, there was a . . . slipway along which cargoes and even small vessels could be hauled, thus saving 200 miles of perilous navigation round the southern tip of the peninsula. In consequence, Corinth boasted two ports, Lechaeum on the Corinthian Gulf to the west and Cenchrea on the Saronic Gulf to the east. Thus "through its two harbors Corinth bestrode the isthmus, with one foot planted in each sea."[2]

Because it was a two-port town, Corinth was a merchant's paradise. All points of the trade compass converged here, so the markets bulged with a worldwide array of exotic goods and rich opportunities. And, as often happens in a wealthy city, opportunities for entertainment, culture, and sensual pleasures abounded. William Barclay explains.

The Greeks had a verb, "to play the Corinthian," which meant to live a life of lustful debauchery. . . . In Greece if ever a Corinthian was shown on the stage he was shown drunk. Dominating Corinth stood the hill of the Acropolis. The hill was not only a fortress; it was a temple of Aphrodite. In its great days the temple had one thousand priestesses of Aphrodite who were sacred prostitutes and who, at evening, came down to the city streets to ply their trade.[3]

Into this city walks Paul, overcome by all the sordid sights and raucous sounds. Certain questions keep haunting him: "How can these people be reached? What can I do? Why should they listen to me?"

An aftershock is quaking his soul.

2. John Stott, *The Spirit, the Church, and the World: The Message of Acts* (Downers Grove, Ill.: InterVarsity Press, 1990), pp. 293–94.

3. William Barclay, *The Acts of the Apostles*, rev. ed., The Daily Study Bible Series (Philadelphia, Pa.: Westminster Press, 1976), p. 134.

Subtle Feelings in Paul

In his first epistle to the Corinthians, Paul himself describes his feelings at this time.

> When I came to you, brethren, I did not come with superiority of speech or of wisdom, proclaiming to you the testimony of God. . . . I was with you in weakness and in fear and in much trembling.
> (1 Cor. 2:1, 3)

Corinth was a low point in Paul's life physically, emotionally, and even financially.[4] But God would not leave His tired servant low and alone. New friends—friends for the rest of Paul's life— await him in this city, as does a dynamic and fruitful ministry.

Paul and the Corinthians

Right away, God begins meeting Paul's needs through a particular couple.

> And he found a certain Jew named Aquila, a native of Pontus, having recently come from Italy with his wife Priscilla, because Claudius had commanded all the Jews to leave Rome. He came to them, and because he was of the same trade, he stayed with them and they were working; for by trade they were tentmakers. (Acts 18:2–3)

At just the right time, God gave Paul just the right people to welcome him. Not only were they fellow Jews, but they also shared the same occupation as Paul. And in testimony to his character, Paul joined right in making tents and didn't once presume upon their hospitality.[5]

The Jews

This trade kept him busy during the week, but on the weekends,

---

4. Apparently, Paul had little money when he reached Corinth, because when he arrived he had to make tents to support himself (Acts 18:3).

5. The word *tentmaker* in Greek can mean "'cloth worker', and it is at least plausible (though not proven) that Paul wove a coarse fabric from the thick goats' hair of his native Cilicia. Called in Latin *cilicium*, it was used for curtains, rugs and clothing as well as tents." Stott, *Spirit, Church, and World*, p. 297.

he was reasoning in the synagogue every Sabbath
and trying to persuade Jews and Greeks. (v. 4)

Week after week, Paul parcels out his time and energy between
working and witnessing. Relief finally comes, though, when Silas
and Timothy arrive from Macedonia—probably bringing an offering
from Philippi that allows Paul to quit tentmaking and begin ministering to the Jews full-time (v. 5; see also Phil. 4:15). However,
the Jews are less than receptive to the idea of Jesus as the Christ.

> And when they resisted and blasphemed, he shook
> out his garments and said to them, "Your blood be
> upon your own heads! I am clean. From now on I
> shall go to the Gentiles." (Acts 18:6)

What is Paul doing here? Giving up in frustration? Giving in
to his temper? Neither, actually. He is merely following Christ's
counsel from Matthew 7:

> "Do not give what is holy to dogs, and do not
> throw your pearls before swine, lest they trample
> them under their feet, and turn and tear you to
> pieces." (v. 6)

Paul had done all he could for the Jews, and still they rejected
the precious pearl of the gospel. So, with a clear conscience, he
very practically said, "That's it!" and turned to the Gentiles.

The Gentiles

Striding out of the synagogue, Paul goes all the way . . . next
door.

> And he departed from there and went to the house
> of a certain man named Titius Justus, a worshiper of
> God, whose house was next to the synagogue. And
> Crispus, the leader of the synagogue, believed in the
> Lord with all his household, and many of the Corin-
> thians when they heard were believing and being
> baptized. (Acts 18:7–8)

At last, a breath of fresh air! No longer stifled by the traditions
of the synagogue, Paul was now teaching in the personable atmosphere of a home—a home in which both Gentiles and Jews were
welcome. Ironically, even Crispus, the synagogue's leader, warmed

to the gospel and linked arms with the Gentiles under Paul's leadership!

Despite this turnaround, though, Paul still can't shake off those feelings of fear and inadequacy; so much so that God comes to him in a vision, saying,

> "Do not be afraid any longer, but go on speaking and do not be silent; for I am with you, and no man will attack you in order to harm you, for I have many people in this city." (vv. 9b–10)

Graciously, God put new courage in Paul through the reassurance of His protection. And not only did He promise His protective presence, He also promised potential growth for the new church. "I have many people in this city," the Lord told him. These promises so encouraged Paul that he shored up his determination and settled for a year and a half in Corinth, "teaching the Word of God among them" (v. 11).[6]

The Opposition and Departure

Their former rabbi gone, a growing number of Gentiles next door, Paul prospering—this was too much for the unbelieving Jews back at the synagogue. So they attack him in the same manner as their counterparts in Thessalonica and Berea.

> But while Gallio was proconsul of Achaia, the Jews with one accord rose up against Paul and brought him before the judgment seat, saying, "This man persuades men to worship God contrary to the law." But when Paul was about to open his mouth, Gallio said to the Jews, "If it were a matter of wrong or of vicious crime, O Jews, it would be reasonable for me to put up with you; but if there are questions about words and names and your own law, look after it yourselves; I am unwilling to be a judge of these matters." And he drove them away from the judgment seat. And they all took hold of Sosthenes,[7] the

---

6. During this time, Paul possibly began his writing ministry, starting with 1 and 2 Thessalonians. Other commentators feel that Galatians was his first letter.

7. Most likely, Sosthenes was the new leader of the synagogue after Crispus. If this is the same Sosthenes of 1 Corinthians 1:1, then he later became a Christian, following Crispus' example.

leader of the synagogue, and began beating him in front of the judgment seat. And Gallio was not concerned about any of these things. (vv. 12–17)

John Stott helps draw out the significance of the court's actions.

> Although it is not certain who is meant by *they all* in verse 17, it seems to be the crowd of Gentile onlookers who, "in an outbreak of the anti-Semitism always near the surface in the Graeco-Roman world" [Longenecker, *Acts*, p. 486], now *turned on Sosthenes*. . . . Luke's addition that *Gallio showed no concern whatever* (17b) does not mean that he was indifferent to justice, but that he considered it judicious to turn a blind eye to this act of violence.
>
> Gallio's refusal to take seriously the Jewish case against Paul or to adjudicate was immensely important for the future of the gospel. In effect, he passed a favorable verdict on the Christian faith and thus established a significant precedent. The gospel could not now be charged with illegality, for its freedom as a *religio licita* had been secured as the imperial policy. Luke's concluding comment is logical: *Paul stayed on in Corinth for some time* (18a), not now because of his vision of Jesus, but because of the judicial decision of Gallio. Jesus would keep his promise to protect him; the chief means of his protection would be Roman law.[8]

You and the Californians

Paul had entered the morally corrupt city of Corinth "in weakness and in fear and in much trembling" (1 Cor. 2:3b). His spirit was shaking, but God was at work protecting him and turning others' lives around. Later, Paul wrote with confidence:

> He has said to me, "My grace is sufficient for you, for power is perfected in weakness." (2 Cor. 12:9a)

As we step back from Paul's Corinthian aftershock, we can jot down three truths about God's sufficient grace in our shaky times.

8. Stott, *Spirit, Church, and World*, pp. 299–300.

First, *the darker the scene, the greater the challenge.* Whether in Corinth or California, where there is little light, there is great need and great opportunity. Second, *the weaker the spokesman, the stronger the message.* Paul came in fear and trembling—too unsure of himself to rely on his own wisdom. So he stayed with the basics, "Jesus Christ, and Him crucified" (1 Cor. 2:2b), which had all the impact he'd ever hoped for. And third, *the greater the resistance, the less the fear.* When resistance grows, we can realize how truly strong the Lord is; and as Paul confidently wrote later: "If God is for us, who is against us?" (Rom. 8:31b).

 Living Insights STUDY ONE

What earthquakes and aftershocks have shaken your life? Here are some examples that rate high on the emotional Richter scale.

• A teacher calls one evening, informing you that your teenage son's grades have been slipping dramatically. The next morning you discover marijuana in his room.

• Your father has become more and more withdrawn from the family. Then one day your mother calls to tell you that he has left her for another woman.

• Your boss circulates a memo stating that layoffs are forthcoming. That afternoon, he calls you into the office and says, "This is not easy for me to tell you . . ."

• Your wife has felt particularly weak lately. After a reluctant visit to the doctor, she receives the test results: cancer.

Are you enduring a life-quake like one of these? If so, write down what is happening.

Paul wrote that he came to Corinth "in weakness and in fear and in much trembling" (1 Cor. 2:3). What are your feelings during this trial?

How did God reassure Paul in Corinth? For example, God gave him Aquila and Priscilla as companions (Acts 18:2). What else did God provide (see vv. 5, 7–10, 12–17)?

_____

_____

_____

As you look back on the past few weeks, has God given you any reassurances? What have you seen?

_____

_____

_____

In an imposing and dark location like Corinth, God started a thriving church, using His weak and trembling spokesman, Paul. What a vivid illustration of God's words to Paul: "My grace is sufficient for you, for power is perfected in weakness" (2 Cor. 12:9a)! How can God's power be perfected in the weakness you are experiencing now?

_____

_____

_____

 ## Living Insights
STUDY TWO

Fear does its best haunting late at night, doesn't it? Surely Paul heard its nighttime tauntings as it reenacted in his mind the angry faces and hateful words he had seen and heard so often before. Because of fear's relentless pursuit, he may have even considered giving up the ministry and vanishing into obscurity.

Maybe that's why the Lord also came to him at night, saying, "Do not be afraid any longer, but go on speaking and do not be silent; for I am with you, and no man will attack you in order to harm you, for I have many people in this city" (Acts 18:9b–10).

Has fear been whispering its dismal messages in your ear lately?

Saying, "You can't volunteer your time at church—your family will never understand. . . . You? A teacher? They'll laugh you out of Sunday school. . . . You can't donate any money—how will you afford the things you want?"

What are your late-night fears telling you?

_____

_____

_____

Suppose God were to speak to you in a vision as He did to Paul. What would He say?

"Do not be afraid any longer, but go on _____

_____

_____."

Paul resisted his fears and listened to the Lord. Won't you listen to Him as well?

BOOKS FOR PROBING FURTHER

The early church has come a long way, from the days when the first Jerusalem Christians dared not venture too far from home, to Paul's latest exploit in Corinth. And along the way it has endured its share of pains—the pain of prejudice and conflict, of failure, of persecution, of legalism, of monumental change. But the church grew through its pain. And in the next study guide in this series, we'll see it strengthen and expand even more.

Before we move on, though, take a moment to reflect on your own Christian growth. Have you endured pains similar to the early church? Has the Lord been stretching you, challenging your prejudices, allowing bits of persecution? If so, consider the list of resources we've provided. They will aid you not only in your further study of the book of Acts but also in your further growth as a believer.

Commentaries on the Book of Acts

Barclay, William. *The Acts of the Apostles*. Rev. ed. The Daily Study Bible Series. Philadelphia, Pa.: Westminster Press, 1976.

Ogilvie, Lloyd J. *Acts*. The Communicator's Commentary Series. Waco, Tex.: Word Books, Publisher, 1983.

Stott, John. *The Spirit, the Church, and the World: The Message of Acts*. Downers Grove, Ill.: InterVarsity Press, 1990.

Studies of the Life of Paul

Bruce, F. F. *Paul: Apostle of the Heart Set Free*. Grand Rapids, Mich.: William B. Eerdmans Publishing Co., 1977.

Longenecker, Richard. *The Ministry and Message of Paul*. Grand Rapids, Mich.: Zondervan Publishing House, 1971.

Disagreements

Virkler, Henry A. *Speaking Your Mind without Stepping on Toes*. Wheaton, Ill.: Scripture Press Publications, Victor Books, 1991.

Wright, H. Norman. *How to Get Along with Almost Anyone.* Dallas, Tex.: Word Publishing, 1989.

Encouragement

Collins, Gary R. *You Can Make a Difference.* Grand Rapids, Mich.: Zondervan Publishing House, 1992.

Failure and Hard Times

Brown, Stephen. *When Your Rope Breaks.* Nashville, Tenn.: Thomas Nelson Publishers, 1988.

Lutzer, Erwin W. *Failure: The Back Door to Success.* Chicago, Ill.: Moody Press, 1975.

God's Will

Smith, M. Blaine. *Knowing God's Will: Finding Guidance for Personal Decisions.* 2d ed. Downers Grove, Ill.: InterVarsity Press, 1991.

Persecution

Brown, Joan Winmill, ed. *The Martyred Christian: 160 Readings from Dietrich Bonhoeffer.* New York, N.Y.: Macmillan Publishing Co., Collier Books, 1983.

Some of the books listed here may be out of print and available only through a library. All of these works are recommended reading only. With the exception of books by Charles R. Swindoll, none of them are available through Insight for Living. If you wish to obtain some of these suggested readings, please contact your local Christian bookstore.

NOTES

NOTES

NOTES

NOTES

ORDERING INFORMATION

Cassette Tapes and Study Guide

This Bible study guide was designed to be used independently or in conjunction with the broadcast of Chuck Swindoll's taped messages on the topic listed below. If you would like to order cassette tapes or further copies of this study guide, please see the information given below and the Order Forms provided at the end of this guide.

THE GROWTH OF AN EXPANDING MISSION

Like watching a beautiful water lily unfurl its petals until it comes into majestic bloom, so is studying the middle chapters of the book of Acts.

Here you'll see the bud of the early church blossom into a worldwide outreach, with the good news of Jesus Christ reaching such cities as free-spirited Thessalonica, intellectual Athens, and voluptuous Corinth. But, like most lilies, you'll also feel the assault of stormy weather and natural enemies as time goes by.

Christ's love will have to overcome prejudice, desertion, conflict, disappointment, abuse, legalism, and endless change—issues that know no generational bounds and still touch our lives today.

If you need the reassurance of God's presence and power in the storms you must weather, or if you hunger for His life-giving touch to open up your life and let it blossom, this study in the book of Acts is for you.

		Calif.*	U.S.	B.C.*	Canada*
GEM CS	Cassette series, includes album cover	$73.47	$68.50	$84.00	$79.80
GEM 1–10	Individual cassettes, includes messages A and B	6.76	6.30	7.61	7.23
GEM SG	Study guide	5.31	4.95	6.37	6.37

*These prices already include the following charges: for delivery in **California**, applicable sales tax; Canada, 7% GST and 7% postage and handling (on tapes only); **British Columbia**, 7% GST, 6% British Columbia sales tax (on tapes only), and 7% postage and handling (on tapes only). **The prices are subject to change without notice.**

GEM 1-A: *Facing the Pride-Prejudice Sindrome*—Acts 10:1–23a
     B: *God Is Not Partial*—Acts 10:23b–48

GEM 2-A: *Getting Out of God's Way*—Acts 11:1–18
     B: *Operation Comeback*—Acts 11:19–30

GEM 3-A: *More Powerful than Prison Bars*—Acts 12:1–17
  B: *Contrasting Lifestyles*—Acts 12:18–25

GEM 4-A: *How God Moves People*—Acts 13:1–4a
  B: *Reaching the Remotest Part*—Survey of Acts 13:4–21:17

GEM 5-A: *When the Going Gets Rough*—Acts 13:4–13
  B: *A Hunger for the Truth*—Acts 13:14–52

GEM 6-A: *Operation Yo-Yo*—Acts 14:1–20
  B: *Wrapping Up a Memorable Trip*—Acts 14:21–28

GEM 7-A: *Grace on Trial*—Acts 15:1–12
  B: *The Essentials*—Acts 15:13–35

GEM 8-A: *When Coworkers Clash*—Acts 15:36–41
  B: *What Opens When Doors Close?*—Acts 15:41–16:10

GEM 9-A: *A Foothold in Europe*—Acts 16:11–40
  B: *Neck Deep in Greece*—Acts 17:1–15

GEM 10-A: *Areopagus Eggheads versus a Seed-Picker*—Acts 17:16–34
  B: *A Corinthian-Californian Impact*—Acts 18:1–18a

How to Order by Mail

Simply mark on the order form whether you want the series or individual tapes. Mail the form with your payment to the appropriate address listed below. We will process your order as promptly as we can.

United States: Mail your order to the Listener Services Department at Insight for Living, Post Office Box 69000, Anaheim, California 92817-0900. If you wish your order to be shipped first-class for faster delivery, add 10 percent of the total order amount. Otherwise, please allow four to six weeks for delivery by fourth-class mail. We accept payment by personal check, money order, or credit card. Unfortunately, we are unable to offer invoicing or COD orders.

Canada: Mail your order to Insight for Living Ministries, Post Office Box 2510, Vancouver, British Columbia V6B 3W7. Allow approximately four weeks for delivery. We accept payment by personal check, money order, or credit card. Unfortunately, we are unable to offer invoicing or COD orders.

Australia, New Zealand, or Papua New Guinea: Mail your order to Insight for Living, Inc., GPO Box 2823 EE, Melbourne, Victoria 3001, Australia. Please allow six to ten weeks for delivery by surface mail. If you would like your order sent airmail, the delivery time may be reduced. Using the United States price as a base, add postage costs—surface or airmail— to the amount of your order. Please use the chart that follows to determine correct postage. Due to fluctuating currency rates, we can accept only personal checks made payable in United States funds, international money orders, or credit cards in payment for materials.

Overseas: Other overseas residents should mail their orders to our United States office. Please allow six to ten weeks for delivery by surface mail. If you would like your order sent airmail, the delivery time may be reduced. Using the United States price as a base, add postage costs—surface or airmail—to the amount of your order. Please use the chart that follows to determine correct postage. Due to fluctuating currency rates, we can accept only personal checks made payable in United States funds, international money orders, or credit cards in payment for materials.

Type of Postage	Postage Cost
Surface	10% of total order
Airmail	25% of total order

For Faster Service, Order by Telephone or FAX

For credit card orders, you are welcome to use one of our toll-free numbers between the hours of 7:00 A.M. and 4:30 P.M., Pacific time, Monday through Friday, or our FAX numbers. The numbers to use from anywhere in the United States are **1-800-772-8888** or FAX (714) 575-5049. To order from Canada, call our Vancouver office using **1-800-663-7639** or FAX (604) 596-2975. Vancouver residents, call (604) 596-2910. Australian residents should phone (03) 872-4606. From other international locations, call our Listener Services Department at (714) 575-5000 in the United States.

Our Guarantee

Our cassettes are guaranteed for ninety days against faulty performance or breakage due to a defect in the tape. For best results, please be sure your tape recorder is in good operating condition and is cleaned regularly.

Note: To cover processing and handling, there is a $10 fee for *any* returned check.

Insight for Living Catalog

Request a free copy of the Insight for Living catalog of books, tapes, and study guides by calling **1-800-772-8888** in the United States or **1-800-663-7639** in Canada.

Order Form

GEM CS represents the entire *The Growth of an Expanding Mission* series in a special album cover, while GEM 1–10 are the individual tapes included in the series. GEM SG represents this study guide, should you desire to order additional copies.

Item	Calif.*	U.S.	B.C.*	Canada*	Quantity	Amount
GEM CS	$73.47	$68.50	$84.00	$79.80		$
GEM 1	6.76	6.30	7.61	7.23		
GEM 2	6.76	6.30	7.61	7.23		
GEM 3	6.76	6.30	7.61	7.23		
GEM 4	6.76	6.30	7.61	7.23		
GEM 5	6.76	6.30	7.61	7.23		
GEM 6	6.76	6.30	7.61	7.23		
GEM 7	6.76	6.30	7.61	7.23		
GEM 8	6.76	6.30	7.61	7.23		
GEM 9	6.76	6.30	7.61	7.23		
GEM 10	6.76	6.30	7.61	7.23		
GEM SG	5.31	4.95	6.37	6.37		
				Subtotal		
		Overseas Residents *Pay U.S. price plus 10% surface postage or 25% airmail. Also, see "How to Order by Mail."*				
		U.S. First-Class Shipping *For faster delivery, add 10% for postage and handling.*				
		Gift to Insight for Living *Tax-deductible in the United States and Canada.*				
				Total Amount Due *Please do not send cash.*		$

Unit Price heading spans Calif.*, U.S., B.C.*, Canada*.

If there is a balance: ❑ Apply it as a donation ❑ Please refund
*These prices already include applicable taxes and shipping costs.

Payment by: ❑ Check or money order payable to Insight for Living ❑ Credit card

(Circle one): Visa MasterCard Discover Card Number_____

Expiration Date_____ Signature_____
We cannot process your credit card purchase without your signature.

Name_____

Address_____

City_____ State/Province_____

Zip/Postal Code_____ Country_____

Telephone (___)_____ Radio Station____ ____ ____ ____
If questions arise concerning your order, we may need to contact you.

Mail this order form to the Listener Services Department at one of these addresses:
Insight for Living, Post Office Box 69000, Anaheim, CA 92817-0900
Insight for Living Ministries, Post Office Box 2510, Vancouver, BC, Canada V6B 3W7
Insight for Living, Inc., GPO Box 2823 EE, Melbourne, VIC 3001, Australia

Order Form

GEM CS represents the entire *The Growth of an Expanding Mission* series in a special album cover, while GEM 1–10 are the individual tapes included in the series. GEM SG represents this study guide, should you desire to order additional copies.

Item	Unit Price Calif.*	U.S.	B.C.*	Canada*	Quantity	Amount
GEM CS	$73.47	$68.50	$84.00	$79.80		$
GEM 1	6.76	6.30	7.61	7.23		
GEM 2	6.76	6.30	7.61	7.23		
GEM 3	6.76	6.30	7.61	7.23		
GEM 4	6.76	6.30	7.61	7.23		
GEM 5	6.76	6.30	7.61	7.23		
GEM 6	6.76	6.30	7.61	7.23		
GEM 7	6.76	6.30	7.61	7.23		
GEM 8	6.76	6.30	7.61	7.23		
GEM 9	6.76	6.30	7.61	7.23		
GEM 10	6.76	6.30	7.61	7.23		
GEM SG	5.31	4.95	6.37	6.37		
					Subtotal	
	Overseas Residents *Pay U.S. price plus 10% surface postage or 25% airmail.* *Also, see "How to Order by Mail."*					
	U.S. First-Class Shipping *For faster delivery, add 10% for postage and handling.*					
	Gift to Insight for Living *Tax-deductible in the United States and Canada.*					
					Total Amount Due *Please do not send cash.*	$

If there is a balance: ❏ Apply it as a donation ❏ Please refund
*These prices already include applicable taxes and shipping costs.

Payment by: ❏ Check or money order payable to Insight for Living ❏ Credit card

(Circle one): Visa MasterCard Discover Card Number _____

Expiration Date_____ Signature_____
We cannot process your credit card purchase without your signature.

Name_____

Address_____

City_____ State/Province_____

Zip/Postal Code_____ Country_____

Telephone ( ) _____ Radio Station____ ____ ____ ____
If questions arise concerning your order, we may need to contact you.

Mail this order form to the Listener Services Department at one of these addresses:
Insight for Living, Post Office Box 69000, Anaheim, CA 92817-0900
Insight for Living Ministries, Post Office Box 2510, Vancouver, BC, Canada V6B 3W7
Insight for Living, Inc., GPO Box 2823 EE, Melbourne, VIC 3001, Australia

Order Form

GEM CS represents the entire *The Growth of an Expanding Mission* series in a special album cover, while GEM 1–10 are the individual tapes included in the series. GEM SG represents this study guide, should you desire to order additional copies.

Item	Calif.*	Unit Price U.S.	B.C.*	Canada*	Quantity	Amount
GEM CS	$73.47	$68.50	$84.00	$79.80		$
GEM 1	6.76	6.30	7.61	7.23		
GEM 2	6.76	6.30	7.61	7.23		
GEM 3	6.76	6.30	7.61	7.23		
GEM 4	6.76	6.30	7.61	7.23		
GEM 5	6.76	6.30	7.61	7.23		
GEM 6	6.76	6.30	7.61	7.23		
GEM 7	6.76	6.30	7.61	7.23		
GEM 8	6.76	6.30	7.61	7.23		
GEM 9	6.76	6.30	7.61	7.23		
GEM 10	6.76	6.30	7.61	7.23		
GEM SG	5.31	4.95	6.37	6.37		
					Subtotal	
		Overseas Residents *Pay U.S. price plus 10% surface postage or 25% airmail. Also, see "How to Order by Mail."*				
		U.S. First-Class Shipping *For faster delivery, add 10% for postage and handling.*				
		Gift to Insight for Living *Tax-deductible in the United States and Canada.*				
		Total Amount Due *Please do not send cash.*				$

If there is a balance: ❑ Apply it as a donation ❑ Please refund
*These prices already include applicable taxes and shipping costs.

Payment by: ❑ Check or money order payable to Insight for Living ❑ Credit card

(Circle one): Visa MasterCard Discover Card Number_____

Expiration Date_____ Signature_____
We cannot process your credit card purchase without your signature.

Name_____

Address_____

City_____ State/Province_____

Zip/Postal Code_____ Country_____

Telephone ( ) _____ Radio Station____ ____ ____ ____
If questions arise concerning your order, we may need to contact you.

Mail this order form to the Listener Services Department at one of these addresses:
Insight for Living, Post Office Box 69000, Anaheim, CA 92817-0900
Insight for Living Ministries, Post Office Box 2510, Vancouver, BC, Canada V6B 3W7
Insight for Living, Inc., GPO Box 2823 EE, Melbourne, VIC 3001, Australia